THE HOME
SECURITY
HANDBOOK

THE HOME SECURITY HANDBOOK

D. G. CONWAY

howto books

Published by How To Books Ltd
3 Newtec Place, Magdalen Road,
Oxford OX4 1RE, United Kingdom
Tel: (01865) 793806. Fax: (01865) 248780
email: info@howtobooks.co.uk
www.howtobooks.co.uk

First published 2005
Reprinted 2005
Reprint TW 2006

British Library Cataloguing in Publication Data
A catalogue record for this book is available from the British Library.

Produced for How To Books by Deer Park Productions, Tavistock
Cover design by Baseline Arts Ltd, Oxford
Typset by Kestrel Data, Exeter
Printed and bound in Italy by 🐎 Grafica Veneta S.p.A.

Contents

1 Introduction

We all know that society is less than perfect and that crime could easily touch us all. If you talk to friends and neighbours you will usually find that most of them have either been the victim of crime or know somebody who has. People fear crime, they feel helpless because they think that there is nothing they can do to protect themselves, but that is wrong! There is a lot that the average person can do, to protect themselves, their family and their property. This security handbook will teach you how to perform a security review on various different aspects of your home and property.

Origins of This Book

I first considered writing a security tutorial when I joined friends who were discussing what they would buy if they won millions on the lottery. Most people included the expected fast cars, luxury holidays and big houses, but there was one priority purchase that was common to most of them and which really surprised me. Almost all of them dreamed of using their fortune to buy a 'secure and safe life style'!

They were ordinary people, leading ordinary lives, people who I thought would have no specific security worries. I investigated further because I wanted to know what additional security they thought they needed. I wanted to know what special threats they thought they faced and how they thought sudden wealth would help them to improve their security. Most of their concerns could be listed under two main classifications:

A) Aspects of their lifestyle that I thought were already within their control.

B) Headline-grabbing crimes, which they were very unlikely to encounter.

Basically, people were worrying about nothing, because with the right information and guidance they could make significant improvements to the security of their home and property at minimal cost.

A 2003 survey asked people which were the most significant threats they thought they faced. I selected the following extracts.

What do you worry most about for yourself and your family?

Crime	45%
Health problems	42%
Being unemployed	29%

What have you done in the last 2 years to address these concerns?

Fit smoke alarms	40%
Take more exercise	31%
Fit burglar alarms and locks	27%

That shows me that many people (45%) are worried about crime, but very few people (27%) had taken steps to reduce their exposure to crime! I think that is because they don't know what they can do. This book will teach you how to look at your house and property, and identify potential vulnerabilities, threats and risks. When you have identified them I will propose simple, affordable and achievable countermeasures that the average person can implement to increase their levels of security.

Lack of understanding and knowledge

Crime statistics can be quite worrying, but they can help us too. For example, look at the facts below.

- A burglary takes place on average every 30 seconds in the UK.
- At least 80% of burglars are opportunists, they look for a quick and easy way in and out. Leave the front door open while you 'nip next door' and your wallet or handbag might be gone when you get back home.
- At least 20% of burglars don't have to force entry, they just walk in through open doors and windows!
- About 60% of burglars enter the target premises from the rear – where there is less chance of them being spotted and or reported.
- More burglaries happen during the day than at night. At night it is quiet and there are more people at home to hear and report strange people, noises, lights or breaking glass where they shouldn't be. For that reason most burglaries happen during the day.

That might worry you, but I want to train you to view this sort of information differently – as opportunities to address potential vulnerabilities. When looking at the points above, I found that the last three were really helpful, because they help us to concentrate our limited resources where they will do most good. For example:

- We can stop the opportunist criminal by not giving them an opportunity! Always close the windows and lock the door when you go out, don't leave wallets and hand bags unattended, etc. By realising that opportunist thieves are around us, then taking a second to think about what we could do, we can remove the opportunities for that thief to target us!
- If 60% of burglars enter a building from the back, we should aim to prevent the burglar from getting to the back of our premises. By doing that, 60% of burglars won't even try to break into your house so we have reduced the chance of your house being burgled by 60%!
- If most burglars break in during the day, by making your house as safe as it can be during the day, you will further reduce the chance that your house will be targeted.

That is the end of lesson one! You have achieved something significant already. You and your family are now considerably safer because you have begun to look for lessons to be learned and have taken or will be taking steps to reduce your vulnerability. As you work through this book, you will identify a number of risks, threats and vulnerabilities as well as deciding how you can remove, reduce or avoid them. From the above lessons you may have taken the following steps to reduce your vulnerability to burglars:

- closing doors and not leaving valuables on show
- denying burglars access to the rear of your property
- making sure your house is secure during the day.

If you have introduced these countermeasures, you have probably made yourself 70% less likely to become the victim of opportunist theft and domestic burglary and that's not a bad result considering this is only Chapter 1!

Do you need a high IQ? Do you have to be wealthy? Do you have to be a master carpenter or welder to improve your security? No, best of all, that is as hard as it gets.

Recording Vulnerabilities, Threats and Risks

As you review different aspects of your home and property security, you will need to record any problems you identify. You may develop your own style and method of recording the vulnerabilities, threats and risks; until then you may want to use the 'form' below.

Home Security Review – 49 High Street – 29th Feb 200X

Problem
Two gaps in the back hedge, one behind the garage and one at the end of the fence where children have broken through to collect their balls.

Other information
Children playing on the open area at the side of the house have broken through the hedge to retrieve footballs that have been kicked into the garden.

The local authority are planting trees and prickly shrubs on the open ground to prevent children playing there and improve the look of the area – which means there will be no more ball games there after the end of the month.

Countermeasures
a) Dig out the whole hedge and replace it with a six foot high chain link fence.
b) Plant prickly plants among the hedge plants, making sure to fill in the gaps with them.
c) Leave the hedge as it is but put a chain link wire fence up on the outside of the hedge.

I suggest that you use a new form to record each threat, risk or vulnerability that you identify. This will help you to control and manage them as you gradually resolve them, improving your security.

Give the form a title, as in the example above. Write the 'problem' in the problem box with any further explanation in the next box, as in the example above. Lastly add any possible countermeasures. You may take them from the examples I list in the book, or you may add countermeasures that are appropriate to you. For example in the problem described above, if you were a bricklayer, you might add a possible countermeasure of removing the hedge and building a brick wall along the boundary!

Recording each problem on a new form allows you to:

- Keep a record of all vulnerabilities, threats and risks identified.
- Gradually review and refine your understanding of the problems as you research them. For example, after looking into the problem you may find that the council has decided to erect a fence along the boundary which resolves your problem at no cost or effort to you!
- As you understand the problems better, you will be able to add to and refine the countermeasures. For example, you may find that you would need planning permission to erect a fence and the council will not grant that permission, so your only option is to plant prickly shrubs to repair and reinforce the existing hedge.
- You will be able to review and sort the forms, which will allow you to place the countermeasures in priority order. For example, you may have identified two potential problems, one is the gaps in the rear hedge, and the other is that the front door cannot be locked. I would suggest that repairing the front door is a priority and that the hedge can wait!
- With additional analysis you can select the countermeasures you wish to implement to resolve any problem. By crossing out the discarded counter-measures you will arrive at a record that shows the problem and the selected countermeasure(s), as shown in this example.

Countermeasures

a) ~~Dig out the whole hedge and replace it with a six foot high chain link fence~~. No planning permission will be given.
b) Plant prickly plants among the hedge plants, making sure to fill in the gaps with them.
c) ~~Leave the hedge as it is but put a chain link wire fence up on the outside of the fence~~. No planning permission will be given.

Work through this book, reading each section until you understand the vulnerabilities, threats and risks that you face. When you are sure you fully understand, work through and compile your list of vulnerabilities, threats, risks and countermeasures. Make particularly sure that you note down any additional threats and risks that may be unique and appropriate to your lifestyle. When you identify an *additional* threat or risk, record it, then use the same common sense process to either avoid it, remove it or reduce the impact to an acceptable level.

Definitions

If we have a common understanding and definition of some basic terms, we will be able to make better progress.

Security

Security is the application of methods and procedures that are used to make our lifestyle secure against any vulnerabilities, threats and risks. By applying security appropriately, we will achieve safety!

Vulnerability

A 'vulnerability' is the avenue that a threat uses to reach you and cause you harm. If your front door lock is broken, that is a 'vulnerability'. If you can't shut and lock the front door, your house isn't secure. If you can't secure the house, the contents and people inside can't be protected against any external threats. A broken front door would be easy to identify. The vulnerability isn't always so easy to spot, however. For example, leaving your garden shed door unlocked leaves you vulnerable in several ways.

Threat

A threat is any occurrence that could cause you harm, loss or distress. Threats may be imposed on us by crimes such as theft, robbery, burglary and assault by drunks in the street. Though this book primarily concentrates on threats that could be imposed on us by criminal activity or accident, we will also probably become aware of other threats, such as fire or flood, and we will address them.

Risk

Risk is the extent of our exposure to the threats to which we are vulnerable. Risk can be measured in two ways: either the impact of the threat or the likelihood of falling victim to that threat:

- The **impact** of a threat is a measure of the damage, injury or loss it could inflict if we fell victim to that threat. For example, the impact of somebody throwing a stone at my car is that I might have to replace a window, or get the paint repaired. However, if I was driving at speed on an unfamiliar road and somebody threw a stone at my car, I could crash, destroying the car and being killed. Thus the risk involved in somebody throwing a stone at my car when it is parked is radically different to the potential risk if they threw that stone at my car when I was driving because the impact is different.

- The **likelihood** of a threat is a measure of the frequency with which we are exposed to it and may become a victim of it. For example, you would agree that being targeted by an international gang of terrorists, who plan to kidnap somebody and demand ten million pounds as ransom, would be a major threat. However for me, the likelihood of that happening is so low that I won't be losing any sleep over it. I don't have ten million pounds and any self-respecting international terrorist would know that. I am of no significance to them and anyway the places I go are not the sort of places they would be frequenting while they looked for a victim! Though kidnapping and murder are decidedly unwelcome, because I am not a senior politician, wealthy celebrity or national leader, I am pretty sure they won't be looking for me.

Countermeasures

A countermeasure is something that you can do to improve your safety and security. My aim is to teach you how to identify problems, then how to propose appropriate solutions to those problems. To do that I will discuss potential vulnerabilities, threats and risks then suggest a range of appropriate potential countermeasures. None of the lists I produce are exhaustive; they simply illustrate the problems and possible solutions. The lists will be a guide for you when considering your unique circumstances and lifestyle, but you will need to spend some time identifying your vulnerabilities, threats and risks, then finding a countermeasure that is appropriate to your lifestyle and circumstances.

Generally when you identify a threat, there are four things that you can do about that risk:

- Ignore it and hope it goes away.
- Take action to reduce the risk.
- Take action to avoid the risk.
- Take action to remove the threat – without taking new and unnecessary risks.

For any given vulnerability, threat and risk some options might not be acceptable because of the intrusive impact they will have on your lifestyle. To illustrate that I will use a simple example. Suppose the threat you have identified is shards of broken glass on the living room couch, using the above strategy there are four options in dealing with it.

- **Ignore it** – keep using the living room and hope that nobody gets hurt when they sit on the couch and the broken glass.
- **Reduce the risk** – keep using the living room, but put a notice on the door warning people not to use the couch because of the broken glass. Perhaps you could also push the couch into the far corner of the room.
- **Avoid the risk** – never go into the living room again, which will make absolutely sure that nobody ever gets injured by the broken glass on the couch.
- **Remove the threat** – buy and wear gardening gloves and goggles as you carefully pick up the larger pieces of glass. Use a dustpan and brush to sweep up the smaller pieces. Finally rent a powerful industrial vacuum cleaner and use it to ensure that all traces of the broken glass are removed before anyone uses the living room again.

Though all of the options would work, it is clear that some options are more acceptable and sensible. Some options are unrealistic or foolhardy and the last option is the most difficult to implement; it actually involves some effort and expenditure on your part. As with this example, for every threat and risk, only you know your circumstances sufficiently well to decide what course of action is best for you, or how you can adapt an approach to suit your circumstances. Maybe you live in a mansion with over two hundred rooms, which means that you can realistically afford to adopt option three and avoid it by never going into that room again!

In this example, for most people we can see that the last option 'removing the risk' is the most effective long-term solution, but it asks you to spend some money to achieve it. Knowing your lifestyle and circumstances you are free to adapt the approach to suit your circumstances. Perhaps you can borrow a vacuum cleaner from your neighbour and you can wear your motorcycling gloves to pick up the glass. You already have a dustpan and brush, so all you have to do is to buy some goggles, which will come in handy for other jobs anyway. By understanding the threat, recognising the options and making use of your own skill, experience and knowledge, you can amend a proposed countermeasure to suit your circumstances. Throughout this book, that will be your primary objective.

- To recognise the sort of threats that are out there and how they can affect you and your lifestyle.
- To look beyond the examples listed, to recognise additional or modified threats to which you are vulnerable due to your unusual or unique circumstances.
- To study those threats and to identify how you can remove or reduce the risks.
- To compile an action plan that sets out the actions you have to take in your lifestyle to reduce or remove the risks identified.

• To continually monitor your life, so that you can recognise change which will be a trigger to performing another personal security review, to ensure that your lifestyle remains as safe and secure as possible.

Though this security handbook necessarily compartmentalises your life, in reality various segments of your life will almost certainly overlap. That doesn't pose any real problems for you, because when performing a security review you have an intimate understanding of all aspects of your life.

When you have reviewed your security, you may want to use your new skill and experience to review security for an elderly relative. If you are attempting to perform a review for somebody else, it should be clear that you will need constant access to and a close and detailed understanding of the person and lifestyle of the subject of the review. Without a fairly intimate knowledge of the lifestyle of the subject of a security review, you cannot hope to understand the impact of potential risks and countermeasures or how relevant they may be.

Safety

Safety is the status we all want to achieve. Safety can be defined as a circumstance in which vulnerabilities have been removed or reduced to insignificant levels, and threats and risks have been removed by the application of sensible and affordable countermeasures.

Non-security problems

While performing a security review people often identify 'problems' that are not security related. For example, while checking the garden, we might smell gas behind the garage, so there could be a gas leak there. When checking the greenhouse, we might discover that there are bare electrical wires visible at the back of the greenhouse heater.

Obviously we should not ignore these problems. They are not security related, but they are a potential threat to us so we have to take action. Call the gas company to investigate the potential gas leak and call an electrician to repair the greenhouse heater. Don't lose track of any of these problems; record them with the suggested form or one of your own design.

Review Method

The method I propose is easy to follow. The book is broken down into chapters and sections, where each one concentrates on a different aspect of your lifestyle security.

Stages

A security review is completed in simple stages. This book will teach you how to perform each of these stages.

Stage 1: Review security

You will review an aspect of your security during which you will identify and record any vulnerabilities, threats and risks that you find.

Stage 2: Prioritise problems

When you have finished the review, you will need to prioritise the vulnerabilities, threats and risks that you have identified and recorded. When this is completed, you will have listed them in order of severity, putting those that present the greatest threat to you and your lifestyle at the top of the list, and those that present the least threat at the bottom of the list. This prioritisation process allows you to concentrate on resolving the priority problems, those that will give you the greatest possible reward for your efforts, making best use of your limited resources.

Remember, addressing the highest priority problems as soon as possible will allow you to make the greatest improvements to your personal safety and security.

Stage 3: Define countermeasures

In stage 2 you prioritised the problems to allow you to concentrate on those that offer the greatest threat to your security. In this stage, you take each problem and attempt to identify and define sensible, achievable and affordable countermeasures that will resolve the problem to your satisfaction. You may come up with only one possible countermeasure, or a list of three alternate countermeasures. When you have identified them, record them.

Stage 4: Adopt and prioritise countermeasures

For each 'problem' you should now consider the possible countermeasures that you identified and recorded. That is, look at the options and based on a range of considerations decide which countermeasure(s) you want to introduce. The decision will be based on a range of issues including:

- **Benefit** – try to decide by how much any proposed countermeasure will improve your security. A countermeasure that delivers marginal benefits should *possibly* be shelved while you concentrate on a countermeasure that will deliver greater benefits.
- **Cost** – try to identify the financial cost of introducing each countermeasure. The cost may be easy to identify. For example 'buy a new padlock for the garage door' will cost £15, plus £5 for extra keys to be cut. Sometimes there are hidden costs, which have to be identified and included. For example, suppose you had identified the countermeasure of 'replace the front door' to improve your security. The cost of the door is £325, but that is not the total cost. Fitting the door will cost an extra £125; new lock, letterbox, handles and house numbers will cost £75. The price of the door and fitting includes a new doorframe, which means the wall around the door will have to be plastered and painted at a cost of £55. So there is a hidden cost of an extra £255 to replace the front door!
- **Resources** – if you are paying somebody to introduce the countermeasure you will just ask for three independent quotes, and pick the quote that offers best value, which may not be the cheapest! As with any purchase, you should also consider reputation and recommendation, quality, availability and your feelings. When dealing with tradesmen and craftsmen, I always consider my 'gut feelings' about them. No matter how well they may be recommended, no matter how low they may bid, if I just don't trust them or I feel there is something not quite right, I won't use them.
- **Degree of risk** – you should also consider the level of risk you will be taking by not introducing a countermeasure. For example, if you don't fix the lock on the front door, you may as well leave the front door open because the lock is useless. That would be a critical factor to be considered when prioritising your countermeasures.

Stage 5: Implement

When all of the decisions have been made, you need to implement the selected countermeasures in the order you decided upon. The countermeasures may be simple, such as shutting the kitchen window instead of leaving it open for the cat to come in when it is cold or wet. It may be more involved, such as cutting back all of the hedges and shrubs around the back of the house then planting prickly bushes to stop burglars hiding there. It could even be life changing, such as changing your job and moving to live in a safer area, while making the children change schools.

This is the most vital stage of the process, the time when you act to protect yourself against the vulnerabilities, threats and risks that you have identified during the lifestyle security review process.

Review Pace

The sooner you review your security and implement countermeasures, the safer you will be, but don't rush the process. Take your time to read each section of this book carefully. Think about each problem that is discussed and consider how that problem or others like it could affect you. When you fully understand them, you will have a valuable insight into the way apparently inconsequential, innocent acts, omissions and decisions could put your security at risk.

When you have finished reading this book, using the examples and descriptions given and your intimate knowledge of your unique lifestyle, you will be able to identify and prioritise the specific problems that could turn you into a victim. More importantly, you will have learned to look at everyday situations and be able to identify where new risks and threats lie, which will allow you to take steps to avoid them. Knowing that not only allows you to make changes to reduce or remove your exposure, it also allows you to continually review your life, identifying and avoiding new threats as they occur.

What You Will Need

To understand and be able to perform an effective security review, you need:

- This security handbook and the methods and explanations contained within it.
- Constant access to and a close and detailed understanding of the person and lifestyle of the subject of the review. Which means you can easily review your own lifestyle, you could review a close family member but almost certainly couldn't effectively review the lifestyle of a total stranger.
- Time to read the book, to consider the range and type of threats discussed and

to take more time to think through and identify how any of the issues raised could affect your particular lifestyle.

• The ability to decide on the relevance and threat level to your lifestyle of the risks discussed, while taking a broader view to decide if you are subject to other more specific and unique threats and risks.

• A notepad and pencil or other means of recording vulnerabilities, threats and risks as you discover them, as well as assigning appropriate and possible countermeasures. The skill, finances and resources to implement any counter-measure that you select.

Other than that there are no specialist skills of knowledge required to be able to perform a security review!

You must:

• Recognise and understand that there are threats and risks all around us.

• Accept that some of your activities will make you more vulnerable and hence at a greater risk of becoming a victim.

• Learn how to identify potential threats and risks in 'your world'.

• Learn how to identify acceptable and possible countermeasures that you can use to reduce or remove your exposure to those threats and risks.

• Remain alert to your surroundings, particularly in relation to some of your activities and actions.

• Become equally aware of the activities and behaviour of the people around you, and be prepared to take action to avoid developing or potential risks.

When To Do It

If you have never reviewed your home security, review it as soon as you can. After that, you should perform a formal lifestyle security review every 12 months.

However, during the year you should remember to maintain an awareness of your world and continually monitor your lifestyle, because a change in circum-stances could invalidate previous reviews and countermeasures.

If you identify a significant change in your life, you should at least undertake a partial security review, but the more significant the change, the more reason there is to perform a new and complete security review! When you have a potentially life-changing experience, you should perform a new lifestyle security review! For example, if you:

- move house
- start a new job
- take a different mode of transport to work – e.g. train instead of driving
- have a child
- come into some money.

It's Your Decision!

Remember that this is general advice. Laws change, and people differ. You may have a totally different lifestyle to everyone else in the country. You may have strange allergies, a love for dangerous sports and a pet tiger! Because there is only one you, this has to be just advice and you must treat it as such. *You* must decide if you want to act on any of this advice. *You* must select actions that are appropriate to you. *You* must check with relevant experts to make sure that you do the right thing for you.

2 House Security Review

You may live in a house, flat, maisonette, apartment, detached mansion, cottage, villa, mobile home or terrace. Whatever you call it, this chapter explains how to review and improve the security of the place you live and for simplicity, we'll call it your 'house'.

Your house is a critical element in your safety and security for many reasons. For example:

- You are often in your house for upwards of 10 hours every day.
- You expect your house to be safe, which means you probably let your guard down when you are there.
- You are in bed and asleep in your house and therefore particularly vulnerable for an average of eight hours each day.
- You rely on your house to shelter your loved ones and keep them safe.
- Your house is often your biggest investment.
- You use your house to store all of your possessions, particularly when you are not at home.

For all of these reasons and more, you have to ensure that your personal security relating to your house is as tight as you can reasonably make it. I accept that you don't want to live in a fortress, but using common sense and a little knowledge you can take steps that will make your house as safe as it can be without making it into a prison.

Though all houses are generally the same, shared accommodation and student digs present some unique problems. There are differences between a detached house and a tenth-storey flat, but all 'houses' have common elements. They all have access points, neighbours, doors and windows, approaches and a perimeter. Surveying the security of a detached house, which has gardens, garages, outbuildings and sheds, is considerably more complicated than surveying a flat because for example, with a flat, you can usually ignore the process relating to fences, gardens, sheds and other outbuildings.

Therefore for the purposes of this book I describe the process necessary to complete the most complicated review and that is for a house which is a semi-detached two-storey building. That house will have gardens, neighbours, garages, greenhouses, sheds, easy access via ground floor doors and windows, potential access to first floor windows, and flat roofs, etc. In comparison, completing a survey on a tenth-floor flat will be easy.

Some flats do have a garden or garage associated with them so you will have to read and understand the whole process and apply what is relevant in your case. When you have read each chapter, apply the appropriate approach to your accommodation.

Remember, when you have learned how to do it, some elements of this security review method could also be used to review the security of a property you are considering buying or renting!

The sub-headings below describe various issues that you can address to improve security and reduce threats and risks in your house.

Research Before Buying

The first part of your survey for the house you live in, or perhaps more importantly for one you are thinking of buying, is to do some research. Try to find out about the area, look for information about crime rates, threats and risks in the area. Look for anything that could adversely affect the security of a property or the people living there. When buying a house most people will check to see if a motorway is planned to run through the garden, or if the local airport management is planning to build a new runway past the greenhouse, but few people check on the security aspects of a house! I have listed a number of sources of information that are available to you to start you off.

Estate agents

The local estate agents could be worth talking to. It is their business to know the area, know the properties and to be familiar with the status of an area, which will affect the price no matter what the property is like. Of course, it is their job to sell properties so you have to find one you can believe! Try an open question such as 'I'm thinking of buying a house in the area – what's the Forest Park area of town like?' (Or whatever area of your town you are interested in.) They should answer even if it is in estate agent talk. For example they could describe Forest Park in estate agent speak where the English translation is as listed below:

- up and coming = shabby and run down
- basic accommodation = a mud hut with an outside toilet
- scope for improvement = a dump that needs a fortune spent on it
- middle class = overpriced small houses
- new development = no character or a noisy building site
- student area = loads of noisy parties
- stockbroker belt = you can't afford it.

Try talking to two or three estate agents. If all of their replies make you feel that it would be safer to move to a war zone, look elsewhere.

Neighbours

Ask around the area, carefully. Local shopkeepers are good sources of information in more ways than one. If you find that the local newsagent shop is reinforced as though they were expecting an armed assault, remember that they did that for a reason! If they have CCTV cameras, steel shutters, serious alarm systems and bullet-proof glass at the counter, you don't have to be Einstein to guess why they invested so much money in their security measures.

You could get chatting to older residents, as long as you remember that they often appreciate the company and may keep you talking for some time!

The objective is to get chatting and listen to what comes out. Don't ask leading questions. If you say something like 'Is there a lot of crime around here?' they will say yes. If you say something more neutral such as 'It seems to be a nice quiet area around here', you will tend to get a more balanced response. For example they may say 'Yes it used to be, until that night club opened. We haven't had a decent night's sleep in nearly two years!'

Remember, what the local people say is only one element in the evidence that you are gathering to build up a full picture of the crime levels in the area.

Insurance Companies

Talk to the insurance companies; they are in business to make a profit. It is therefore in their interests to know which areas have a higher crime rate, as they charge higher rates in high crime areas than they do in low crime areas. It is worth talking to your insurance company or insurance agent and asking them for a quote **17** to insure a house of a similar size and value to your current house but in the area you are interested in. If where you live now your detached three bedroom £159,000 house costs £295 to insure for building and contents each year, and a similar house in the new area will cost £875, there has to be a reason. If they charge three times the rate, it may be that there is three times the risk in that area.

Talk to them. They may give you inside information – it may be crime but it could just as easily be flood or subsidence from old mine workings. Ask why the difference, but be aware of other reasons for differences in quotes. They may have mistakenly quoted for a thatched house when yours has concrete tiles. They may not have allowed for an introductory discount, which you are getting from your existing company. They may have included uninsured loss cover, new for old and a host of other extras that can have a huge effect on the quote. Talk it through, and understand what they are quoting and why.

Local authority

The local authorities are worth talking to. They know what happens in each area – they have to repair damage caused by vandals. They know how many problem families they have in each estate and they know where they have to regularly send the teams of workers to clean up drug taking debris.

Be honest and ask them outright. Ask if they have any reports describing crime rates and the cost of vandalism, etc. Some council managers are officious and obstructive, so if you don't get an answer out of them, talk to some of the council staff!

Local newspapers

Buy the local newspapers or even visit their offices or the local library and scan through back issues. Local newspapers carry local news, exactly the sort of information you need. Vandalism, muggings, robbery, burglary, arson, assaults and any other crime you care to mention.

Taking an hour or two to check through back issues of the local newspaper will not only tell you what vulnerabilities, threats and risks you would face if you moved there, it could also give you an idea of crime trends. For example, as the local criminals get older, over a couple of years you might see a reduction in vandalism and an increase in street robbery and burglary!

Schools

You could try to make contacts at the local school; they would be well aware of the youth crime trends because they deal with the youths responsible for those crimes on a daily basis. If you have children, you want to know what the schools in the area are like anyway, so while you are there extend your questioning to crime in the local community.

Local community police officer

It may be worth talking to the local community beat police officer. What you would like them to say is 'Don't move into that road – the whole family at number 27 are criminals, Mr Jones at number 16 has convictions for violent crime and there is a drug dealer living in number 34.' But of course, due to confidentiality issues they cannot tell you that. Apart from the legal issues, police forces generally will not allow their employees or officers to give advice about different areas. However, if you were to say you were thinking of moving into a house in Badger Road, then ask – as a friend – if the police officer would be happy to live there, I doubt if anyone would object to that. If they then replied that personally 'I would never buy a house in Badger Road', you can draw your own conclusions from that.

Environment Agency

In some areas, if not all, you should check with the Environment Agency to make sure that the house you are looking at is not subject to risk of flooding. On the Environment Agency website, you can type in a postcode and check flooding maps, which will give you a good idea of the risk of flooding for any given location and property (www.environment-agency.gov.uk).

Internet sources

Various other Internet sources are available for you to make your checks as well. Some local authorities and other organisations hold information about crime rates and trends. For example www.crimestatistics.org.uk holds information that you can search on a postcode basis.

Make a note of any relevant information that you find during your research. If you were thinking of moving into an area, the results of this survey may be all you need to decide to look elsewhere.

If the general crime levels are acceptable, there may be other areas that you will need to be aware of, for example because of increasing vandalism and petty theft.

Make a note of the problem areas and concerns and carry them forward to your house and possessions survey. You went to a great deal of trouble to find this information, use it!

House Security Survey

The most important way of improving the security and safety of your house is to perform a home security survey.

If you are proposing to undertake a security review of your house, go ahead and survey it.

If you are proposing to review security for a house owned by a close relative, make your arrangements and do it. I suggest that you do not try performing a security survey on a house you are thinking of buying until you have performed at least two or three other security reviews because lack of practice and the restrictions placed on you by lack of full access can invalidate the results.

If it is a house you are thinking of buying, you will have to discuss it and make arrangements with the current owner. You won't be able to go into as much depth, so you will have to rely to a large extent on what the current owner tells you and will have to move quite quickly.

House Survey – External

Your first task is to undertake an external security survey of the area around the house. Read each section thoroughly, then when you think you are ready, take a notepad and complete an external security survey. If necessary remind yourself of the basic details needed to record the vulnerabilities, threats and risks you identify.

No matter where you live, the procedure is the same, but circumstances will change the content and scope of the external survey. For example, if you live in a 15th floor flat you probably won't need to look at fences and garden tools. I say probably not – but when you have seen the relevance of boundaries and garden tools to your personal security, you may wish to keep that in mind and include a check for similar threats. For example, there may be a cycle cupboard on the landing outside each flat, or a cleaners' or maintenance store on each floor – those cupboards are the equivalent of your fence and garden shed!

The objective of an external survey is to stand back and take a close look at the house and the immediate surroundings. You should make a note of any vulnerabilities, threats and risks that you identify. As you list them you should take a few minutes to consider and list any justifiable and workable countermeasures. The example threats and countermeasures described below should help you to think along the right lines, but never forget that you have a unique lifestyle. You know your lifestyle and you are the best person to recognise dangers relevant to you and to identify appropriate, justifiable and achievable countermeasures.

Area

Walk around the surrounding area. Walk along the main access routes that lead to your house and make a note of the impression you get. Is it for example 'general light industrial units with some residential'. Perhaps your area is 'run down and shabby residential', or maybe 'affluent commuter belt'.

When you tour the area with an open mind, the impression you get is the impression that the rest of the world gets when they approach your house. With a little consideration it also gives some useful pointers in relation to the security of your house. For example, though the interpretations are rather stereotyped, different appearances could mean different things:

Industrial means lots of people from 9 am to 6 pm Monday to Friday, deserted after that and also deserted on weekends and bank holidays. Therefore with no witnesses around a burglar would be free to pursue his trade at those times.

Shabby Residential depending on circumstances may mean several things. It could mean a community in decline, where they have little community pride so litter and vandalism are commonplace. It could just mean that the local authority has not yet implemented their refurbishment plan for the area or that the dustmen are on strike. Shabby residential could indicate high unemployment, which could mean alcohol and drug problems, which could mean high crime rate because the residents need to get their money from somewhere to feed their drug habits. It is only an indication though – it could just as easily reflect the recent closure of a major employer or bad budgetary management and incompetence by the local authority.

Remember, at the moment we are gathering general evidence, so keep an open mind. You should also remember that your knowledge of the area in which you live will give you an insight. You could always talk to people as you survey the area and see what additional information and 'feeling' they give you. Be careful what you say, of course, don't offend or upset people by being too blunt or asking too many questions. Aim to be conversational and wait until later to write down anything that they tell you.

I was doing a commercial security survey once minding my own business, wandering around with a hand-held dictation recorder, when two large gentlemen approached me aggressively. It took a few minutes and some blunt comments from them for me to realise that they thought I was investigating fraudulent benefits claims, and a few more minutes for me to explain I was doing a commercial property survey.

Affluent Commuter Belt means large well-kept houses, equals wealthy residents with a lot of valuable possessions. Commuter belt might mean successful husbands at work leaving houses from 8 am until 6 pm each weekday, wives potentially at home. Worth a thief watching to see when the residents come and go. It could be worth breaking in just to see what is available. Large gardens, possibly containing valuable statues (some easily worth £1,000 each), garden machines (ride-on mowers worth up to £5,000 each), pond life (specimen carp worth up to £3,000 each). Large and mature gardens, designed to give the tenants privacy, at the same time shield the approach and work of a burglar. Large bushes and hedges could hide a burglar from passing traffic as he breaks a window and even mask the noise of the breaking glass. Wealthy means maybe two holidays per year, which is at least four weeks each year when there will be nobody at home at all (worth coming back with a van for that garden equipment – if anyone asks 'we're taking it for service'). Could also mean expensive cars left outside every night, some with valuable contents! Down side: probably alarmed (though false alarms are so frequent that often alarms are ignored and anyway drunks and drugged criminals might just ignore the alarm bells and carry on thieving).

New starter homes means young residents starting out on the property ladder. Probably both out at work though Mum might be at home with a new baby. Young and trendy so they may have latest electronic goods and gadgets, could be worth breaking in. Down side: starter homes packed closely together, small gardens, no mature plants and hedges, so criminal activity would be easily overlooked, heard or spotted.

Rural means a mixture. Some smaller homes – worth taking a look for money and portable valuables, some large estates packed with antiques. Most large country homes tend to have an alarm, but some don't. Even if they are alarmed anyone responding to it will take at least five minutes to reach the property. (Don't go breaking into large rural homes though – many of them have early silent alarms so the police will be there before you've got in the window.)

Rural properties of any size frequently have a range of outbuildings – offering a range of easily accessible valuables, from garden machines to vehicles, expensive horse tack (e.g. saddles and bridles) to sporting equipment (e.g. skis and fishing equipment), pedigree animals to tool boxes. Little passing traffic and no close neighbours are a huge benefit to a burglar. The down side is the possibility of advanced alarm systems, CCTV and deserted roads! If the burglar is unlucky, a passing police patrol may stop him and ask why he is on a remote country road at two in the morning with a van full of garden machines, saddles and electric tools!

Look for signal crime.

As you walk around look out for vandalism, fly tipping, graffiti, broken glass and other petty crime. This is called 'signal crime' because it is a signal in several ways:

- There are criminals active in the area.
- There could be a lack of pride in the community and therefore an unwillingness to speak out against and prevent crime.
- Criminals will read it as an invitation to indulge in their own crime. Generally, where there is visible crime, there will also inevitably be more serious crime that is not apparent to a casual observer. Some see signal crime as the first step on the slippery slope to total lawlessness and decay.

Look to see who is around.

As you walk around you should also be looking to see who is moving around in the area. Unfortunately criminals don't wear badges or uniforms so you are not likely to be able to spot 'criminals', but you can get a feel for the type and numbers of people you come across.

Just as people mature, communities tend to mature as well. A new estate is built and young families move in. They have children, so Dad leaves for work then each school-day morning the mums and kids leave the area to walk or drive to school. Later on the mums come home alone and the cycle repeats itself in reverse soon after three in the afternoon.

As the community matures, the children grow up and leave home, so generally parents live alone, the school run stops but the commute to and from work remains. For a really mature community you could expect little early morning activity because most of them are retired. There might be a flurry of activity each Tuesday when they all go to the post office to collect their pensions but otherwise the pattern of movement has become a pattern of no regular movement!

By observing who is around you could identify times of greater risk to you and your property. For example generally with a young community your house will be fairly safe between 8.30 and say 10 in the morning. During those times there are too many people moving around and as criminals don't want to be witnessed and reported they will not be active in that area.

On the other hand, if you live near the local football stadium you might find that after the match on a Saturday drunken louts spill out of the stadium in unsociably high spirits. Having drunk too much, they vandalise cars and gardens and assault people as they move towards the railway station to go home.

Drunken louts – countermeasures 1

✔ If this were the case, your sensible countermeasure would be to park your car elsewhere on a Saturday, lock the gate, don't go out when the match is finishing and don't leave anything valuable in the front garden.

✔ If the antisocial behaviour and crimes peak after each football match you should report it and demand that something should be done. You will need evidence to support your claim so you would also be advised to log crimes in the street, and complain in writing to the stadium, the local police and the local authority while copying the complaint to the local MP. Supporting that complaint with a petition from residents would carry more weight.

Sometimes residents find that they live on a route which is habitually used by drunks. Consider a poorly managed public house that is located at the end of a dead end street. Clearly all of the pub's customers would have to travel down that street to arrive; more significantly, at closing time they would be ejected from the pub late at night and have to travel back up that street when they leave the pub. In such circumstances it is common for residents to be plagued by petty crime and disturbance almost every evening.

Drunken louts – countermeasures 2

✔ I would suggest residents make a log of all incidents and log any calls made to the police and their response. With a few months of recorded evidence I would then make a formal complaint to the police, the landlord, the local licensing authority and copy it all to my MP.

✔ Properly identifying patterns of movement and the type of people moving around at different times will help you to accurately assess threats and risks in a given area.

Approaches to your house

When you have completed your review of the area in which you live, you need to review *all* approaches to your house. For example, a single house on a straight road that runs north to south has two basic approaches – from the north and from the south.

The approaches are important to you. You need to identify them and review them to perform a thorough security review of the property. You will have to walk along each approach and with your 'criminal's eye' try to identify any actual or possible vulnerabilities. For example, walking along from the north you realise that pedestrians, including a passing burglar, can see into your lounge, where your new plasma screen TV, video camera, stereo system, top of the range home computer and laptop computer are waiting invitingly. He will also be able to see that there is nobody there on the ground floor. Other things that can be seen in an approach are:

- easy entry points and easy exit carrying your valuables
- low or broken fences
- unlocked sheds with expensive tools and equipment
- workshops and garages left open that allow the burglar to take a convenient inventory of what is there to be stolen
- expensive patio and lawn furniture
- expensive statues, urns, birdbaths and other garden ornaments
- ponds containing expensive specimen carp
- aviaries with expensive exotic birds
- greenhouses with expensive propagators and heaters
- garden tools (spade or fork) that can be used to force a window or door
- ladders left outside which will give easy access to roofs and windows
- any signs of any dog, or a burglar alarm
- any signs that the resident is disabled or elderly, such as wheelchair ramps and handrails
- any vehicles associated with the premises.

Visible vehicles

The vehicles visible can tell us a lot about the people who live in the house. For example, there is a transit van and a Ford Focus, so we know that the man of the house is an electrician because we can see the 'Jackson's Electricians' van in the front drive. He almost certainly works on customer sites from 9 am to 5 pm. He probably has a lot of valuable tools and equipment in the van and garage, not to mention that interesting looking locked shed! Looking into the Focus as we walk past we can see a baby seat strapped permanently onto the front passenger seat, and a pair of low heeled women's driving shoes left in the driver's foot well. So, the Focus belongs to Mrs Electrician and she has a baby!

Our burglar can read your property as easily as that. He will walk or take a drive by and will read all of this and more – that is why you have to identify and review all approaches to your house.

Other possibilities

It isn't often as easy and straightforward as that, however. The example we used above is simple, but now suppose that the house is on a corner plot. The presence of the side road gives us a few more approaches. The possible approaches are now:

- from the north
- from the south
- coming out of the side road and turning south
- coming out of the side road and turning north
- coming from the north and turning into the side road
- coming from the south and turning into the side road.

You should identify, walk, drive and review all approaches to fully understand what can be seen and what that might indicate to the passing burglar. As you recognise and add new access routes, the possible pattern of approaches can get very complicated. Spend a few minutes thinking about the variety and number of possible approaches for the new house described below.

- It is situated on a major crossroads.
- There is a petrol station forecourt to the left of the property.
- There is a public footpath running along the right-hand boundary.
- The public footpath leads to a public playing field at the rear of the property.
- There is pedestrian and vehicle access on all sides of the playing field.

Now assume it isn't a house but a flat in a tower block, where people have to and are allowed to walk along the balcony within inches of your front door and open kitchen window. What about the country cottage, very picturesque but on a quiet country lane surrounded by open fields?

As you should be able to see, you can soon generate quite a long list of possible approaches and access routes to most properties. Because they are places where the burglar might approach your house, you should be aware of them, and have checked them for possible vulnerabilities.

I spoke to a senior scenes of crime officer who told me that he considered the following properties to be the most vulnerable to intruders and burglars.

- corner plot
- house with public footpath running down one side
- houses by playing fields, parks or other public areas
- end of terrace houses

Is anyone in?

Criminals do not usually want to be disturbed, witnessed or caught in the act. Though some burglars almost specialise in entering premises while the residents are asleep upstairs, generally to avoid being caught burglars prefer to carry out their crimes in empty premises. If there are clear signs of occupancy most criminals will walk past and look for another property to break into. After all, why should they take an increased risk when there are so many other more vulnerable targets just a short distance up the road?

Your objective is to take as many steps to protect yourself as you can justify, each of which will make your house just that bit harder to break into. Your aim is to reach the point where the burglar will decide that the obstacles and risks are too great and so he will pass on by looking for an easier target.

To illustrate this point, ask yourself one question. If you were a burglar faced with two houses, one has an alarm, a large dog, stout fences, prickly bushes inside the fences, and people seem to be moving about in several of the rooms, while the other house has none of those things, which house would you target?

Obvious clues

As mentioned above, most criminals would prefer to target empty premises. Some of the signs are clear, and can almost be an invitation to a burglar. For example, if it is after dark and you see a house with no lights on, the gates to the drive open, the garage open with no car inside, do you think the homeowner is out? If the car is missing we can be pretty sure that the residents are out and that they left the gate and garage open so it will be easier for them to drive into the garage when they get back. Unless they are sitting quietly in the dark, there is nobody at home, so should they be surprised if they come home to find they have been burgled?

Even if the homeowner wasn't so obvious with the clues, it is amazingly easy for a criminal to find out if somebody is in – they just knock at the front door! If nobody answers they know that nobody is home so they are free to slip around the back and help themselves. If somebody does answer the door, the criminal will say something like 'Does Jack the mechanic live here?' You say no and close the door and the burglar goes away. He doesn't care because there are plenty more vulnerable houses down the road!

There have even been cases where helpful neighbours have assisted criminals, for example when a neighbour saw somebody knocking at the door of a house and helpfully said something like 'Mr and Mrs Jones are in Brighton visiting their daughter, they won't be back until Tuesday!' Guess what Mr and Mrs Jones find when they get back on Tuesday.

Is anyone in? Countermeasures

✔ Tell a friendly and trustworthy neighbour that you are going to be away.

✔ Consider leaving a contact number with them in case of problems.

✔ If you will be away a few days consider leaving the number of a nearby relative who will be able to act as keyholder if the neighbour thinks there is a problem.

Finding your house

When you are performing your survey consider the identification of your house and how the emergency services will find it in an emergency. If you live at 10 Badger Road finding your house is quite easy. As a police officer I know where Badger Road is and maybe know that the numbering starts at the junction with Fox Lane. I can easily drive into Badger Road and shine a torch at a house. If I see that the house I am looking at is perhaps number 20 and the next house is number 19. I simply accelerate and drive a few houses down knowing that I will soon be at the front of number 10 Badger Road!

Now consider how difficult that same process will be if the residents don't like house numbers. The residents have decided to use house names instead of numbers so I am now looking for 'Woodpeckers' in Badger Road. Where is it? I have no idea. In the worst possible case I will have to drive along the whole length of the road looking at house names until I find 'Woodpeckers'. Even then, as a police officer I have attended named houses where the owners have allowed the sign to become overgrown or to fall down. Just to make it harder, some house names are fixed to gate posts, some to gates, some on poles inside the grounds, some fixed to the front of the house. Some are carved into wood, some painted on metal and some in little plastic letters screwed to moss-covered brickwork.

Testing it out

Check your house at night in the rain to see how easy it would be for the police, fire brigade or ambulance service to find your house. To get a really unbiased view, discuss this with a colleague at work and offer to do a trade. Select somebody who doesn't know where you live and then agree to meet them one dark and stormy night. When they pick you up, sit quietly in their car and watch them try to find your house. Don't say a word, just monitor how easy or difficult it is for them to find it. Don't give any hints or tips and don't make your house stand out by for example turning all the lights on or leaving your white BMW in the drive – they will know your car if they see it every day at work. See how long it takes them actually to park outside your house, that will give you a feel for how hard it is for the emergency services to find you when you most need them.

You might be surprised at how long it takes and if it does, remember that all the time your friend is looking for your house it could have been on fire, or somebody lying ill inside or a burglar running riot. Don't forget to return the favour and try to find your colleague's house to give them an idea of how easy it is to find it.

Next, imagine you are a police officer, ambulance driver or firefighter, who doesn't know where it is and you have to find it in an emergency. Where do you look for the nameplate? Which side of the road is the house you are looking for? Reviewing the identification of your house will pay dividends.

Finding your house – countermeasures

✔ If possible, arrange to number all houses in the road in sequence so it is easy to find them.

✔ If houses have names only ensure that the house names are clearly visible and easy to read.

✔ Explain the problems and ask the residents' association to consider standardising the location, style and positioning of house names on houses in your road. For example 'reflective white background, black lettering, situated to the left of the gates at a height of about six feet from the ground'.

✔ If your house only has a name and you call the emergency services, help them find you by describing the location. For example, 'From Fox Lane, turn into Badger Road. When you pass the wooden bus shelter on the left-hand side we are the next gateway on the right, it has white painted brick gateposts.' The radio operator should relay the instructions so help will arrive quicker.

✔ If emergency services have been called, if it is safe you could send somebody up to the road and tell them to wave a torch or do something to attract the attention of the emergency services. If you do, tell the operator what you have done, for example, 'they will see a man in a green anorak at the gates, he will be waving a torch'.

Front view of your house

Stop at the front gate and spend a moment looking at what you can see with your 'criminal's eye'. Imagine you are a thief or vandal and try to see what seems open and available to you. Make a note of vulnerabilities. For example:

- unlocked or open garages, sheds, greenhouses and other outbuildings
- open windows and doors in the main house
- convenient ladders left beside the shed that will make getting in easier

- flat roofs with easy access to second floor windows (upper floor windows are almost always less secure than ground floor windows).
- vehicles
- signs of dogs (not welcome)
- signs of burglar alarms such as bell boxes or signs saying 'these premises are protected by . . .'
- visible signs of goods worth stealing, e.g. televisions, CD players, digital cameras, computers, etc.
- indications of lifestyle and patterns (for example, a works van missing means he is out at work, children's toys mean mum probably does school runs each day).

When you have identified everything you can see, you have a ready-made list of simple, effective and free or inexpensive countermeasures. The following are just examples; you should be able to identify and list more countermeasures appropriate to your house and lifestyle)

Front view – countermeasures

✔ Always lock garages, sheds, greenhouses and other outbuildings.

✔ When you go out make sure all windows and doors are closed and locked.

✔ Remove and securely store ladders and other tools and equipment that could be stolen or could be used by criminals to break into your house. Remember a spade or shovel is quite effective at prising a door or window open.

✔ Take steps to secure access to flat roofs, make sure that any second floor windows accessible from flat roofs are as secure as they can be, and post signs (even if you have them made up) saying that the premises are protected. It at least shows a criminal that you have taken action to protect your property.

✔ Make vehicles as secure as you can. Put the car in the garage even if you are going out later the same day. Make it harder for the criminal to 'read' your property, so they don't know if the absence of a car means you are out or just that the car is in the garage and the whole family is actually in.

✔ When you are out, try to leave some lights on and leave a radio tuned to a talk station – not music. Eavesdroppers will only hear voices and hopefully assume people are inside talking so they will move on.

✔ It may be worth putting up a 'beware of the dog' sign, or leaving some dog toys on the patio even if you don't have a dog – check in the local charity shop!

✔ Invest in a burglar alarm. They can be very expensive, but some are quite reasonable. The best are monitored, which means that the alarm company has an office that is manned 24 hours a day, where all alarms are monitored by their staff. When an alarm sounds the staff call the police. Some companies provide dual burglar and fire alarm systems; they will call the appropriate emergency services depending on the alarm activation. It is possible to buy dummy alarm boxes and dummy CCTV cameras. Career criminals will be able to see that they are not real systems, but the dummies might be real enough to put off an opportunist thief.

✔ Blinds or net curtains at windows will reduce visibility for criminals. If they can't see who if anyone is inside and what valuable goods there are, they are less likely to enter premises, especially if they can see that you have taken other countermeasures to prevent theft and other crimes.

✔ Some signs of lifestyle patterns you cannot hide, such as a works van in the drive or the school runs, but you can deliberately break that pattern occasionally. For example, leave the van at home and take the car to work if you have a day of meetings or a training course. Co-operate with other parents and sometimes collect each other's children too, or ask grandmother to sit at home and be deliberately visible while you are off taking or collecting the children.

The purpose of all of these countermeasures is to make you and your house a less tempting target. Try to remove all indications of vulnerability, and introduce as many indications of anti-crime measures as you can. Every step you take is one step closer to making the criminal walk past to look for an easier target.

Frontal access

In this section you are concentrating on looking at access. Frontal access to the property is quite important. It has been known for criminals to bring a removal lorry and clear a house of anything of value. Others have driven into a property in broad daylight and loaded an expensive car onto a breakdown truck and driven off with it.

If the criminal doesn't have access they can't commit a crime! You cannot build a 20-foot high concrete wall topped with electrified razor wire, but you can reduce access to an acceptable level.

Check the access to your property and make it as secure as you can, bearing in mind:

* **Planning requirements** – check to see what you are allowed to do.
* **Ease of access** – for genuine visitors, deliveries and emergency services.
* **Aesthetics** – though you may get planning permission for a ten-foot high chainlink fence along your front boundary, will the neighbours be happy about it and will you like living in what looks like a prison camp?
* **Cost** – will the cost of the measures you are considering be justified by the increase in the levels of security and peace of mind you will get from the work?

- **Value** – can you justify the cost of the work against the value of the premises? For example, if you own a cottage valued at £200,000, is it sensible to spend £300,000 making it more secure? Would you be better off moving and combining the money you get from the sale of the cottage with the money you would have spent on making it more secure, then buying a new house that is already more secure. (You can use this review method to help you select your new house.)

Frontal access – countermeasures

✔ Erecting fences and locking side gates will deny criminals easy access to the rear of the property.
✔ Locking the gates to the drive will prevent anyone from easily taking a vehicle in or out of the premises without your permission.
✔ Siting the pedestrian gate under a street lamp and ensuring that the footpath to the front door is unshielded by bushes will also improve security levels by exposing anyone approaching the house to public gaze, as well as making them more visible to occupants of the house.
✔ Depending on the location and conditions, consider installing lighting that may be operated by a switch, timer or automatically triggered by movement sensors. A criminal will not want to be floodlit while he tries to attack your property.

Fences

Check the boundary. You might have fences, hedges, walls or no boundary obstruction at all on some open plan estates. Tour the boundary of the property, and make a note of the type of boundary and the condition it is in.

The general rule is that you should have high fences at the back of the property to stop the criminal getting in. Once out of sight at the rear of a property a criminal would be free to take his time to find or make an entry point. If fences and gates prevent him from getting to the rear of the property he is less likely to target the premises.

At the front you should have lower fences so that a criminal or other intruder will be visible to neighbours and passing traffic if he attempts to enter your premises.

We are not in the business of designing gardens; our objective is just to make the property as safe as we can, as quickly as we can, with minimal effort and at a reasonable cost. Our aim is not to turn the property into an unapproachable fortress; it is to take *reasonable steps* to secure the property to the point that a criminal will see our countermeasures and walk past to look for an easier target.

A property is safer if anyone passing has an uninterrupted view of the front of the property. If they could be easily seen by anyone who walks or drives past, a criminal is less likely to attack a property. Fences and gates can be scaled or broken, but if there is a clear view to passing traffic the criminal is less likely to attempt to gain access to the rear of the property.

Points to note

Remember that you may need planning permission to erect fences and walls. Before you do anything, approach your local council planning office and discuss your proposals with them; they should offer valuable advice.

You should also remember that you have a duty of care and should not allow or cause harm to anyone on your property, whether they are a legitimate visitor or not (Occupiers Liability Act 1984).

Walls

Brick, block or concrete walls are very strong, but unfortunately they are sometimes a blessing to a criminal. Criminals might quite like your nice tall strong wall, because it gives them stout foot and hand holds to let them safely climb up and over. While they are outside, a wall protects criminals from dogs or easy surveillance from anyone inside the property. But once the criminal has climbed over, the wall now offers him good protection from surveillance and discovery by the public who may be passing by outside. Then, when he has finished raiding a property, the criminal can use the wall to hide from passing traffic, until it is clear for him to make a getaway with your valuables.

Expensive burglar alarm systems, approved and legal anti-climbing paint and spikes, etc. can deter the dedicated burglar. Walls will usually stop a passing opportunist thief or vandal, because they want to be in and out quickly and easily and a wall or fence will slow them down.

Wooden fences

Not as strong as a wall, they can be quite solid, flimsy or anything in between. Wooden fences are not as expensive as a wall, but they usually require more maintenance effort. They can be climbed, but a determined criminal will simply kick or cut a hole in even the strongest wooden fence.

Wire fences

Can be cheaper still and available in a variety of heights and styles. They can be topped with strings of barbed wire in some circumstances and they can also be alarmed, but that is an expensive option. Wire fences will deter a lot of intruders, especially if topped with barbed wire, but they have one fundamental weakness. When installed even on level ground, it is easy to scrape a hollow under the wire and slide through. To prevent that, wire fences can be installed with buried 'aprons', concrete footings and stakes set into the ground, but that makes them a lot more expensive. Whatever preventative measure you take with a wire fence their ultimate flaw is that anyone with a pair of wire cutters in their pocket can get in. Worse still, if someone cuts a vertical slice through the wire fence behind a bush or tree, a hole can remain undiscovered for weeks.

Metal Railings
Expensive to 'very expensive'. Spiked railings are probably the most secure fencing there is, which is why they cost so much. The foundation required for some railings can also prevent access underneath, unless the criminal is going to do an awful lot of work to dig through. A hacksaw and plenty of time is needed to cut through railings, or a noisy and expensive mechanical cutter. A hole in metal railings is usually quite easily spotted. Again alarms and sensors can also be fitted to give an added level of protection but they are very expensive options.

Hedges
Rural in appearance, and favoured by people who don't want to feel that they live in a prison. They range from cheap, decorative and ineffective, to expensive and impenetrable. Hedges are not as unsightly as some metal and wooden fences, so they may appeal to people on aesthetic grounds. They will prevent casual intrusion because they form a barrier. Select the right shrubs and with correct care, watering and pruning of the plants they will form a dense and to a large degree impenetrable barrier. Weaknesses are drought, disease, pruning shears and fire. Drought and disease can destroy a hedge in weeks. Fire can destroy a hedge in minutes. A single intruder with a set of pruning shears can cut an access point in minutes. They can be expensive to buy and plant. They usually take months if not years to reach maturity and therefore provide a real barrier. Cost of maintenance is therefore high, and the protection offered is variable. Prickly plants offer better all round protection, but if you have young children, you may decide that the prickly plants may be an unacceptable risk to the children.

Open Plan
A legal requirement on some properties, aesthetically pleasing to many and uncomfortably exposed to some. Open plan is quite common on more modern estates. Boundaries are sometimes marked by a few marker posts; other than that there is no barrier between properties or between public and private areas. It is

obviously a cheap option. Some deeds and tenancy agreements specify that boundaries must be erected and maintained, while others specify that no boundary fences are allowed. Security against intrusion is non-existent, but the open plan nature does mean that a criminal will be totally exposed as he creeps around a property.

Fencing – countermeasures

✔ **Combination boundary**. This is the most common approach used. By combining some fencing and boundary styles you can increase the level of protection they give – for example, a chain-link fence with prickly hedge planted on the inside of the fence line. The chain-link does not have to be so effective because the deterrent of the prickly shrubs acts as a more worrying deterrent to the criminal. The prickly hedge does not have to be so expensive or carefully tended as a stand-alone hedge, because the chain link fence is the primary barrier, the hedge is a secondary and painful deterrent. The roots of the hedge also quite effectively prevent an intruder from digging underneath the fence wire.

✔ **Insubstantial trellis**. Quite a sneaky and inexpensive countermeasure. By applying an insubstantial or weak trellis to the top of an existing fence or wall you will deter most intruders. Aesthetically it is not unattractive, particularly when trailing and flowering plants can be grown through it to 'naturalise' it and reduce the visual impact. (Though you should take advice from the gardening centre or fencing contractor. Heavy growth on fast growing climbing and trailing plants combined with strong wind will wreck your trellis.) Flowering plants are quite a good barrier and reduce the enclosed feeling of bare walls and fences. On a cost basis, trellis is quite cheap to buy and fairly easy to install. It will deter an intruder because they know that if they try to climb over the wall with the trellis on top, the trellis will break. That means they may fall and be injured. Breaking the trellis and falling will make a lot of noise, which could attract the attention of neighbours or people passing by, so the police could be called. For that reason a wall or fence with a trellis on top is usually considered a no go area for a criminal.

✔ **Add noise makers**. At modest cost it is possible to add alarms or noise makers to a boundary. For example, stretch thin lines attached to tins which contain a handful of gravel along the barrier. If an intruder tries to climb the wall he will catch the line, pull it and make a noise. When the noise starts he will quickly be gone to avoid detection and capture. However you should remember that 'traps' that are designed and set to injure intruders are illegal and using them could put you in court or even prison. It is possible to get electronic alarms that work off trip lines, or alarms that are triggered by intruders breaking light beams, but they become quite expensive and difficult to set, because birds, cats and wildlife will often set them off. A householder may decide to install them along one particularly vulnerable fence line, but I urge a very careful calculation of cost and benefit before taking that route. I did see one householder who had used cheap personal attack alarms. They cost about five pounds each, they were about the size of a cigarette packet, and were triggered by pulling a line that removed a pin to set off the alarm. To stop the alarm you had to remove the battery, or find the pin and push it back into the hole. He had them set up in a wooden shelter like a bird nest box on top of a wall, where an intruder would pull a line and remove the pin by climbing over the wall.

✔ **Security patrols**. You could pay a security company to patrol your property. Some companies offer silent monitored alarms and patrols while others offer simple mobile patrols checking your premises at various times during a day and/or night. The cost per household of this option can be very high, though prices can be pulled down if residents group together and pay for an entire street or area to be patrolled. The security company will erect signs and have a visible presence in the area at different times of the day and or night.

✔ **Cheat**. You could simply erect signs saying 'Beware! Guard Dog' or 'Premises Patrolled By XYZ Security'. A motivated professional burglar will not be put off, but a passing opportunist thief might be. You have to weigh the cost of signs and dummy alarm boxes against the benefits you will get and make your choice.

Gates

Any fence almost always has to have at least one gate built into it. The fence then becomes as good and secure as the gates that have been installed. Gates should be as secure as any section of fence, but they also have to be simple and convenient for authorised people to unlock them, open them, use them and secure them again afterwards.

No matter how good a gate is, because it is designed to allow access through a fence or other barrier, it is a weak point. There are a number of design criteria and considerations that must be taken into consideration when erecting fences and gates.

Gate – countermeasures

✔ Don't install a gate unless it is absolutely necessary.
✔ Generally, the smaller the opening in the fence and the smaller the gate the more secure the fence or barrier will be.
✔ Gate posts and frames should be stronger than the surrounding fence posts, because they have to take additional strain from opening and closing of the gates and knocks while in use.
✔ Hinges should be secured to prevent intruders from simply lifting a gate off its hinges.
✔ Gate locks should be as solid and secure as locks on a door, preferably with a two point locking system to distribute the load and stress on the gate and gate post.

Paths

Footpaths can add to the security of a property, or at least the positioning and construction of footpaths can. I doubt if anyone could walk on a gravel path without making a noise during the day, and at night the sound of somebody walking or even sneaking over gravel sounds like an express train passing. If you lay a gravel drive and a gravel path surrounding your house, it acts like a mediaeval moat, preventing unwanted visitors from approaching the house without announcing their presence by walking over the noisy gravel.

Remember, when considering these countermeasures you don't have to adopt all of them immediately. You can keep some countermeasures in mind and use them later on at appropriate times. For example, though your current house does not have a gravel path, when you consider moving you could look for a house with gravel paths because you know that will be an additional layer of protection.

You can also keep some countermeasures in mind and possibly introduce them later when the opportunity presents itself. For example, if the gas company engineer wants to dig up your driveway to lay a new mains pipe, you could agree, but ask them to lay a gravel drive when they fill in the trench!

Given a choice build a path that takes a direct line from the gate to your front door. Don't make a path that meanders around the property giving a criminal an excuse or opportunity to do anything other than come and go to the front door. Try to avoid putting the path across the front of the house, especially if it will give visitors the opportunity to walk past and look into windows. Don't let them look in to see who is or is not at home, and don't give them the chance to look in to see what is worth stealing.

Feel of the property

Now you have had a chance to check the property over from out on the street, try to think like a criminal. What is your feel for the property? I will use two extremes as examples to illustrate what I mean by your 'feel' for the property.

- **Open House**. The open house is a criminal's delight. Quiet road with little or no passing traffic, windows left open and with a spare front door key under the doormat. Family members are careless, they come and go leaving the front door unlocked and open, there are cars with valuables in clear sight and keys have been left in the ignition. Gates left open, lots of unattended overgrown shrubs and bushes in the garden, the fences are broken down leaving a dozen ways in and out. From the street we can see unattended valuables, handbags, cash and wallets, no pets, no alarm and apparently no idea of how to protect themselves or their property.

37

- **Fortress**. The fortress has strong secure fences, and prickly shrubs, side gates that are locked with no view of or access to the rear. They have two German Shepherd dogs, which are loose inside the house and back garden. The house is alarmed, windows and doors clearly protected by professionally installed locks. There are gravel paths and a gravel drive, with sensor-operated flood lighting. From the street we can see no valuables at all. The residents are obviously very careful and meticulous about household security.

Given these two properties, if you were a criminal which house would you target? Hopefully you would walk past the 'fortress' and head for 'open house'. Having taken a while to look at your property, given a scale of 'open house' to 'fortress', where do you think your property stands?

You now have a 'feel' for the impression your house is giving people who pass by. Carry on with the survey but keep your impression of the property in mind. If your house is closer to open house than fortress, criminals will be taking a greater interest in it, so you have to work harder to bring it closer to the fortress assessment.

Back garden

Explore the gardens or grounds of the property. Check the side and back fences. What state are they in, what is on the other side of the fence? How easy would it be to get into and or out of the back garden from the side or rear of the property? What access is there across any fields, allotments or other gardens to houses that don't have side gates or fences?

Is the garden cared for? Are there unruly bushes and wild plants in which a criminal could hide unseen? Are there any overhanging branches that could make it easier for an intruder to climb over the fence? What work needs doing to make the garden a safer and more secure environment? Make a note of countermeasures you could take.

Back garden – countermeasures

✔ Repair or replace broken or rotten fences.
✔ Plant prickly hedges as a secondary barrier.
✔ Cut down or trim unruly shrubs and bushes to remove hiding places that a criminal could use.
✔ Trim back any overhanging trees that may help a criminal to climb over any fence you have.
✔ Lock away any ladders, tools, planks of wood or anything else that a criminal could use to enter your property.
✔ Consider installing sensor-operated floodlights.

Children's bikes and toys

This section raises a security issue and touches on behaviour. In security terms, the value of the bikes, toys and equipment children own can be considerable. That being the case they should be valuing their possessions and taking care of them. If the house is secured and the residents are out, you should not be able to see (and easily steal) expensive bikes, or other toys or equipment.

Teaching children the value of possessions is character building. Teaching them to care for their bike and other toys, to respect their own property and to behave in a reasonable way plants the first seeds of maturity, with a balanced view of care, concern, value and respect.

Whether you support that approach or not, you should not be able to see hundreds of pounds' worth of children's bikes and toys laying around a garden waiting to be stolen.

Outbuildings

Many houses have one or more outbuildings. For a complete household security survey you should also survey any outbuildings you may have.

Garages
If there is a garage, walk around it and assess its vulnerability. What is it built of? Bricks or concrete are quite secure, but wooden planks can be cut through or prised off in minutes. Are there any windows? If so where are they located – out of sight at the back or in full view of people passing by? How big are they? Are they big enough to climb through if they can be opened or broken? What sort of doors does it have? Are the doors locked? Are the doors actually secured when they are locked, or is the lock useless? What sort of lock is used? How many locking points are there? With a three point locking system on barn style doors, i.e. bolts top and bottom and a central lock, the door is very secure. Using just one single central lock on the doors allows too much movement; the door can be bounced in and out and that can easily break open a large door.

Can you see what is inside? Is what you can see worth stealing? Could a criminal easily make off with the contents if they manage to get into the garage? (Remember you should always lock your car and put the steering lock on, even if it is in a locked garage.) Out of interest, ignoring any cars, do a visual inspection and add up the estimated replacement value of the contents of the garage. I am sure that the total will surprise you when you add the value of tools and garden furniture, etc. It will make you realise why the garage needs protection.

Description	Make	Model	Serial Number	Unique Marks	Other Information	Photograph
Hammer Drill	Black & Decker	AA34/1v	BD-63859FN	Post code engraved on case and handle	Chuck key tied to cable with plastic string	Video of garage
Mechanics Tool Case	Banner & Jones	Set 456.78	546-4A44	Post code engraved on case and some hand tools		Photo album 2 picture 2 and 3
Gent's Mountain Bike	Mountain Trail	Pro Rider 3	MT-PR3-365498697	Post code engraved on bottom of cross bar	Mostly blue, red flashes on cross bar and sprung forks	Photo album 1 picture 6 and 7

Check the contents of the garage. Do you know the make, model and serial number of the valuable tools etc that are usually kept in the garage? If not, make a note of the details as soon as possible. Use a table such as the one suggested above to record details.

Make a note of any problems or vulnerabilities that you discover in relation to the garage before you move on.

Sheds
If there are any sheds in the garden, perform a similar survey on them. Check the location, construction, windows, doors, locks, etc. Can you see what is in the shed? Do a quick calculation of the estimated replacement cost of the contents of the shed. If it's like most sheds, I think you will be surprised at the value of the goods you have stored there.

Greenhouses
Even greenhouses can contain valuable tools and equipment! Good quality garden tools are very expensive, not to mention propagators, greenhouse heaters, petrol lawnmowers, etc. Check the contents and add up the estimated replacement cost of the tools and equipment stored there. The total soon adds up.

Outbuildings – countermeasures

✔ Check the construction and maintenance (locking a garage with a rotten back wall is a waste of time). Make sure all outbuildings are in good repair. If they are not, don't use them until they are repaired or replaced.

✔ Make sure all outbuildings are always locked.

✔ Make sure all locks are effective and secure.

✔ Keep a note of the contents of each outbuilding, the total value of goods stored there and of course details of tools etc (make, model and serial numbers).

✔ Mark all valuables with your postcode and house number. If you do mark your property display a 'Marked Property' sign at the front door of the house and on the shed, greenhouse and garage door.

✔ Remember that a photograph with some sort of scale in the picture (such as a tape measure or ruler) will be of help if property is lost or stolen.

House Survey – Close Perimeter

A close perimeter survey is the area where you are almost within arm's reach of the house. Criminals are only likely to get that close to your house when you are out. To perform an effective close perimeter survey, you will have to make sure that the house has been locked and secured just as if the residents were all at work or out shopping.

You have already viewed the property from a distance; for the close perimeter survey walk around the perimeter in touching distance of the building, paying particular attention to potential access points and other threats.

Threats and access points to look out for include:

- **Doors** are the favoured access point for most criminals. Pay particular attention to all doors. The strength, fit and locking mechanism should be noted and you should check to see if keys have been left inside door locks – if you break the glass you can reach in to get the key, and with the key you can open the door.
- **Drainpipes and service cables** – giving foot and hand holds to an intruder to climb in through upper storey windows.
- **Solid trellis and climbing plants** – giving access to windows and balconies for an intruder.
- All **windows** should be closely inspected from outside. The strength, fit and

41

locking mechanism should be noted. Also check to see if keys have been left inside in window locks. (You should consider the option of installing laminated or wired glass in any windows that are particularly vulnerable, such as windows in hidden corners or at the rear of the building. The laminated and wired glass is a lot harder to break through, needs more effort on the part of the criminal, takes more time and makes more noise. All of these factors are likely to make a criminal decide to move to an easier target.)

- Check for **hidden corners** where plants or outbuildings could allow an intruder to wait or work unobserved. It is possible that a back door or ground floor window could be positioned in an awkward corner where nobody can see it from neighbouring houses or from the road because of sheds, garages or shrubbery, etc.
- Check for the obvious presence of **phone lines**, which could be identified and cut by an intruder.
- Check the state of the **brickwork, tiles and cladding** which if badly maintained could make it easy for a criminal to gain access.
- Check for access to **flat roof areas**, which could in turn give easy access to possibly less secure windows on upper floors.
- Check for access to **first floor roofs**. I once attended a house where intruders had climbed onto a fence, climbed onto the roof of the house, lifted a few tiles and dropped into the house through the roof! (Fit a lock to the loft door.)
- Walk around any outbuildings such as stables, etc., and perform a similar review on them.
- Check for the presence of **exterior lighting**. Where is it installed, what area does it cover and how is it operated? Remember, if you have a remote property where there are no neighbours to see what is happening, if an automatic light is triggered by a criminal, all you have done is help the criminal by providing him with light while he breaks into your home. Lights are generally only effective where people are at home, or better still where neighbours and passing traffic will be able to see any criminal activity if a flood light switches on.

You may well discover a variety of potential threats that are not strictly speaking security related. For example, you could discover a pile of cardboard and paper piled up against the wooden cladding at the rear of the house. On bonfire night a stray firework could ignite it and block access or exit from the back door of the house.

Keep an open mind and look for any potential access points, threats and risks that could realistically affect you. If after a little consideration you think they are worth noting, record them on your survey form with appropriate possible countermeasures. For example, a large tree with a rotten-looking dead branch that overhangs the footpath at the side of the house is clearly a threat. Make a note of it, and see to it.

Close perimeter – countermeasures

✔ **Drainpipes and cables**. Replace heavy metal pipes with reproduction plastic pipes. They do the same job, look enough alike to maintain the architectural style of the building but are not strong enough to support a climber. Beware of problems with planning permission for listed buildings, or any objections a landlord may have.

✔ **Trellis and climbing plants**. Ensure that trellis is weak and will not support the weight of a person. Some experts say that climbing plants damage a building anyway, because their tendrils eat into brickwork and stonework causing damage to the structure of the building. Climbing plants also harbour moisture and insects and can allow rodents to climb into the property. If sections of the plant die off there is potential for fire damage to the building due to the presence of the combustible dead plant material permanently fixed to the wall. I would advise the removal of climbing plants, or at least their removal in critical areas, including under windows. But it is your wall, your plant and your choice!

✔ **Doors and windows**. If windows and doors are found to be insecure on inspection, you will have to check to find out why they are insecure. Perhaps it was an oversight, or perhaps like one household I surveyed it was stupidity. They said they always left the utility room window open to give the cat access to a warm dry room. I pointed out that the utility room was sited at the back corner of the house and that anything or *anyone* using that window had free access to the rest of the house. Though they knew that, they started shutting the window after we had discussed it!

✔ **Door and window locks**. If windows and doors are secured, performing a non-destructive test will tell you if they could withstand a determined intruder. Grabbing the door handle and gently shaking will tell you if you could force the window or door. Be gentle, no need to destroy the property just to prove that an intruder could do it. By rattling the door or window you can see and feel where there is movement. Perhaps the frame is loose on the hinge side, or maybe the top bolt is not latched – make a note of insecurities, for the action plan.

✔ **Hidden Corners**. If there are potential access points that cannot be seen they are not secure. You could take several steps to overcome this. Such as fitting metal bars in that window, cutting back bushes and trees, or moving a garden shed so that the access point can be easily seen by neighbours or people passing by.

✔ **Phone lines**. I think it unlikely that many people would be targeted by an intruder who was so determined to press home his attack on an occupied premises that he would seek out and cut the telephone lines. With some alarm systems the failure of the phone line actually triggers an alarm anyway. As there are mobile phones in most houses I don't think this would be much of a threat unless you were very wealthy or a public figure. If it is of concern to you, you could shield or hide the phone line, or ask for an overhead connection that is above easy tampering reach.

43

✔ **Brickwork**. Some brickwork is so eroded that it presents enough foot and hand holds for a criminal to climb up to upper floor windows. It has also been known for a criminal to chip a hole in a rotten brick wall to gain access to premises. Apart from the need to maintain the structure of the building, the householder should realise that failing to maintain the brickwork could pose a security threat.

✔ **Flat roof Access**. A flat roof will almost always give easy access to upper floor windows and sometimes to balcony doors, etc. Upper floor windows are for some reason rarely as secure as ground floor windows. People seem to think that upper floor doors and windows don't need to be as secure as ground floor doors and windows, even though there may be fairly easy access. By planting prickly plants around the area with a flat roof you deny easy access to that roof to a criminal. By replacing metal drainpipes with weaker plastic ones, removing climbing plants and sturdy trellis, then mounting anti-climb products around the edge of the flat roof you add another deterrent to the criminal. By ensuring that upper floor windows are as secure as ground floor windows, you will stop the intruder even if he does go to the trouble of climbing up onto the roof.

✔ **First floor roof access** should be restricted as much as possible. The roof is quite vulnerable, so anti-climbing paint, anti-intrusion spikes, etc. will be effective in denying access to the roof – check for planning permission and other restrictions.

✔ **Outbuildings**. Check them for valuable contents, insecure access, ease of access to transport (if the criminal can reverse a stolen van up to your workshop it will make it easier for him to load up and steal your household, DIY and garden tools).

✔ **Lighting**. Consider upgrading, repairing or installing sensor and timer mounted floodlights, but only if the lights will display criminal activity to neighbours or passing traffic.

Remember to make a note of any threats and vulnerabilities, and if possible resolve those vulnerabilities immediately. For example, lock the ladder away now, close the garage door and tell everyone to lock the utility room window (the cat will have to wait outside until somebody comes home).

The external survey should now be complete. You might want a moment while it is fresh in your mind to go back over your records and check the threats, vulnerabilities and countermeasures you have noted. Add any additional explanation you might need. For example 'Cat' might have been enough to remind you that you always leave the utility room window open so that the cat can climb in when he gets cold or hungry. On checking your notes you may decide to add 'Cat – close and lock window' just to be sure you remember that when you have finished.

Please remember that the report you are compiling would be a blessing to a burglar if it fell into his hands. It will list all the vulnerable points on your property and all of the possessions worth taking, so make sure that you keep it very, very secure, and destroy it when you have acted on it!

House Survey – Internal

The internal survey begins to look at the actual security of the premises perhaps checking some of those doors and windows that didn't feel too secure.

To make sure that you check through all the rooms in your home methodically, without missing anything, start at the front door and turn left. Move around each room, beginning on the left, as if your left hand is kept on the wall, turning left whenever there is a gap or doorway.

Adopting this approach you should not miss any rooms. When the ground floor is done do the basement if there is one, then work your way through upper floors surveying each floor using the same method.

Read to the end of this chapter before you start your internal survey. If you don't understand what you are looking for, you may miss important things.

Shared occupancy

Some accommodation is shared, such as boarding houses and student accommodation. For anyone in accommodation with shared occupancy, the security risk is 20 times greater than single occupancy.

With single occupancy buildings, you can lock the door and keep the world outside, with shared occupancy any number of people have access to the building. The smaller the private area that is controlled by the multiple occupancy resident, the higher their security risk. For example:

- In a single occupancy house, you can lock the door and the only persons allowed in the garden, let alone the house, are family members and guests.
- In a shared block of flats, the tenants of 20 other flats, their guests, visitors, delivery men and others can prowl the building without causing undue concern. That means that the front door to your flat is all that is between you and potential criminals.
- As a lodger or in student accommodation, you may share a kitchen and bathroom and only have a single room under your control. That means that your bedroom door is the only barrier between you and the world, and bedroom doors are not usually noted for being solid and secure. Will you always lock your bedroom door if you go to the toilet, or make a drink in the kitchen? It may be an insult to other residents and their guests but you should! Never leave the keys in the door, they could be borrowed and duplicated. Never assume you will only be a minute nipping down to get the post – a conversation

with the postman may delay you for five minutes which is plenty of time for your wallet, cash, credit cards, watch and camera to go missing!

- In some cases you may share one room with several people! With friends and relatives, partners, lovers and visitors wandering around shared occupancy your security barrier is you. You can only guarantee security when you are in the room and awake; other than that you can only guarantee security of items that you carry with you at all other times.

Shared occupancy – countermeasures

✔ Be aware of the problems associated with multiple occupancy.

✔ If forced to share insecure accommodation, carefully consider the wisdom of buying and keeping any portable valuables in your room.

✔ Consider buying a solid lockable steel cabinet, which you can use to store valuables while out of the room.

✔ Never leave money, credit cards, etc. unattended and in view even for a minute.

✔ Consider leaving your more valuable property with relatives if your shared accommodation is particularly vulnerable.

✔ Make sure that you keep records of property serial numbers, etc.

✔ Try to foster a security spirit among fellow residents in shared accommodation. For joint safety and security agree that everyone should always lock the street door, never let anyone in who you don't recognise (even if he says he is 'a friend of Baz on the top floor'), most important, *anyone can and should challenge strangers*, particularly:

  ➤ anyone who is not recognised by residents

  ➤ anyone who looks flustered or surprised

  ➤ anyone carrying or removing anything from the premises (don't believe them if they say they are taking the DVD and television or laptop computer for repair).

Fire

It is important to remember that fire is a threat as well. You are already committed to undertaking an internal survey, so it would be sensible if you also took the time to do a fire safety assessment of the home at the same time.

I am not an expert in fire safety. If you are in doubt, local fire and rescue services will sometimes come to do a fire safety check on the premises. The following common sense checks should be useful, but make a note of anything you find in relation to any unique threats and hazards you find relating to your premises.

Smoke Detectors

Smoke detectors can be battery or mains operated. They can be independent, where each unit sounds an alarm if and when it detects smoke, or they can be linked, where all units sound an alarm if any of them detect the presence of smoke. The linked system is clearly more expensive and more difficult to install, but independent units can usually be installed by anyone with a drill and a screwdriver.

Some expensive monitored burglar alarms also include smoke detectors. They are wired into the system, and if a smoke detector is triggered the alarm company will often call to check with the householder that they have not just burnt some toast or opened the back door to let smoke from a bonfire into the kitchen! If the householder doesn't answer, or confirms that there is a fire, the alarm company will call the fire and rescue services, even if the householder has already done so.

Smoke detectors can contain just the detection and alarm units, but for a small additional cost you can obtain a smoke detector that has a built-in emergency light which operates when the alarm is triggered. The 'emergency' lighting can be a big help when trying to evacuate at night to help people get out in a hurry.

When installing any smoke detectors, make sure that you follow the siting and installation instructions on the packaging. Experts can advise on the number and positioning of smoke detectors, but as the battery units are so cheap and so easy to install, I always install one in every room, plus light alarms at the top and bottom of the stairs and inside front and back doors. In that way, wherever a fire started, I am assured that alarms will soon sound even if one or two units failed. To me the bottom line is that a handful of smoke detectors is a cheap way to protect my family.

When doing the internal survey of each room, take a moment to check for the presence of smoke detectors.

Smoke detectors – points to note

- Check to see where they are sited and if they have batteries in them.
- Make sure that you test the smoke detectors by pushing the test button at least once each week.
- Make sure that the batteries or the unit is changed if the test fails, and if they still fail replace the unit and the batteries.
- Make sure that the batteries are changed on all units once each year. The easy way to remember to change smoke detector batteries is to give them the same birthday as yours. That way when it's your birthday, buy a new battery as a present for each smoke detector, then you shouldn't forget.

Check for threats

Take an extra moment to check for fire threats in each room. There are hundreds of potential threats. A few example threats are described below.

Some paraffin heaters are poorly maintained and leak paraffin. Some are badly positioned, for example being placed at a point where people often have to squeeze past, or on an upper landing where they can get knocked over and where any fire will cut off the escape route to people on the upper floors.

To dry laundry indoors in poor weather, people are sometimes tempted to put washing too close to a heat source to accelerate the drying. Unfortunately the closer they put laundry to a fire or heater, the greater the risk of a fire.

Some people use electric or other heaters, and try to get the most heat out of them by placing them as near as they can to where they are sitting or sleeping. A badly positioned heater can soon ignite bedding, curtains or armchairs causing a serious and life threatening fire.

Electrical wiring

Old wiring can be a threat. Most people rely on an increasing number of electric appliances to make their life comfortable, to help them with their work or to entertain them. All of those appliances need a source of power, all of which has to be drawn through the existing wiring in a house. It is surprisingly easy to overload these circuits. Imagine a modern teenager's bedroom, where we could find a television, hi-fi system, computer and associated printers, scanners and modems, not to mention a separate computer games console! Now what if there are two teenagers and add on Mum's hairdryer – how much power do you think that circuit can supply before it blows a fuse, melts or bursts into flame?

Occasionally you will still see single sockets, with multiple adapter blocks plugged in so that half a dozen or more plugs can be plugged into and supplied with power from one socket. You are more likely to see extension leads with an adapter block capable of taking two, four or six plugs all running off one wall socket. Sometimes extension leads are daisy-chained and plugged into each other to run a dozen computers, hi-fi systems, televisions and computer game consoles. All of that use potentially overloads a single socket and could cause a fire. As a rule of thumb, if there are not enough sockets for all of the appliances you want to use – the house needs rewiring to bring it up to a standard where you can safely plug all of your appliances into sockets that have been installed by an electrician.

If you are surveying a house that you are considering buying make a note of trailing cables and multiple plugs in a single socket. They are an indication that the wiring is not adequate, which is a leverage point to bring down the price and make a reduced offer.

From 1 January 2005, people carrying out electrical work in homes and gardens in England and Wales will have to follow the new safefy rules in the Building Regulations. Visit www.odpm.gov.uk/electrical safety for more information.

Electrical wriring – points to note

✔ Assume that any electrical device should be plugged into a wall socket that has been installed by a qualified electrician.

✔ Trailing cables, extension leads and adapters are all signs that a house does not have enough sockets. If there are not enough sockets it was probably wired a long time ago. In any case, it probably needs rewiring. (If you are thinking of buying the house – ask when it was rewired and reduce your offer by the price of rewiring.)

✔ In the UK it is recommended that the electrical wiring in a domestic residence should be professionally tested at least every ten years – get yours tested.

✔ Remedial work that is disclosed by any tests should be done as soon as possible. The tester will condemn and disconnect any wiring that is dangerous!

Cigarette smoking

Insurers have been known to increase the insurance fees payable by smokers for life, health and property insurance. Worst of all, cigarette smoking is the cause of house fires that kill hundreds of people. About one third of fire-related household deaths in the UK are attributed to smoking and smokers are nearly twice as likely to have a house fire! If you cannot eradicate smoking from your house, make sure that the fire risk is minimised by taking steps to ensure that cigarettes do not cause a fire. Remember, the fatal Kings Cross station fire and the fire in the Mont Blanc road tunnel were caused by discarded cigarettes. Careless smokers kill!

Smoking – points to note

- No smoking in bedrooms (falling asleep with a burning cigarette will set bedding alight).
- No smoking in the lounge (falling asleep or forgetting a cigarette can cause armchairs and other soft furnishing to catch fire).
- No smoking in the garage (there may be fuel or other flammable material stored there).
- To be really strict without actually banning smoking, follow the example of a lot of companies and designate a smoking area. That may be outside the back door, or it may be in the greenhouse in wet weather. Both areas are 'safe', so smokers can be requested to pursue their habit in those areas for the safety of the rest of the family, which isn't a lot to ask.

Household rules

By establishing standing rules and procedures in your house you will increase your security. The purpose and benefit of rules should be explained, discussed and agreed by everyone in the house, because the rules will benefit everyone who lives there. Though you should set your own rules to meet your own unique circumstances, they could include:

- Never leave electrical appliances on when they are not attended.
- Never smoke cigarettes in the house (or at least in bedrooms or living rooms).
- The last person to leave the house will make sure all windows and doors are locked.
- Smoke detectors will never be disconnected, or have their batteries removed (to be used in portable CD players or portable games consoles, etc.)!
- Smoke detector batteries will be replaced on the birth date of the head of the household, or before if weekly tests show that the batteries have failed!
- When preparing meals, cooking pans will never be left unattended.
- Valuables and other property will never be left on show in an unattended car.
- Cars will always be locked when left unattended.
- Car keys will never be left in an unattended vehicle even for a minute.
- Inform local relatives or close friends if you are going to be away from home for more than a day or so.

Practice escapes

Most people do not realise how disorienting a dark and smoke filled environment can be. You think that you know your way around your house and could evacuate under any circumstances, but take away the light, add smoke and a little panic and things look a lot different. As a police officer I was invited to attend BA (breathing apparatus) training with a fire crew, and was totally disoriented when the lights went out and the practice smoke filled the practice house. (Smoke is toxic so they use harmless 'practice' smoke in their exercises.)

To be ready, I suggest that you should practise escapes, especially in houses where there are younger children. When only adults are involved, it is easy to introduce more realistic conditions. For example, doing it at night and declaring 'fires' at various points in the house, checking to make sure that people leave by a 'safe' route.

You could also blindfold an escapee to mimic the disorientation of darkness, smoke and heat. Blindfold the person, turn them around a few times and then tap them on the shoulder, which is the signal to escape. If you do try this method, each blindfolded person must have a minder at hand. The minder will check to make sure that the blindfolded and disoriented evacuator doesn't try to walk off a balcony or flat roof, or otherwise injure themselves or damage anything. Remember that nothing will be as disorienting as a real fire, but blindfolded evacuation can be dangerous if minders are not in place.

Practice escapes with children
With children it is more difficult, as you have to maintain their trust in you and their feeling of safety within the home. Don't push too hard and don't scare them. Though you have serious intentions, make it fun, make it a competition and 'grown up' game for younger children. Award them prizes for remembering what to do and doing it right.

You could start by sitting and gently explaining what you are going to do. This is easiest after they have had a fire drill at school, because they then know that this is something that people do sometimes. Start by asking them to tell you how they did it at school, then tell them you want to see how clever they are and how quickly they can get out of the house if there is a problem. Start gently by sitting in the lounge and tell them the competition has started and that they must get out and stand by the front gate or wherever you define as your meeting point.

Remember that **nothing** is more frightening and disorienting than a building on fire. People will leave by the nearest available exit and you want to know if they are all out. The only easy way of doing that is to agree a meeting or rally point where everyone who gets out of the building gathers. Then it is easier for the leader to check who has escaped and who may still be inside the building – so you can report that to the fire services when they arrive at the scene.

With children's practice evacuation, offer them plenty of praise and support to encourage them. (Older children can skip ahead to more realistic exercises.) Make

51

sure that the children are rewarded – chocolate, a trip to the cinema or their choice of day out, anything that reinforces the exercise as a pleasant experience and nothing to be worried about.

When the first exercises have been successfully completed, increase the complexity. Get them to lie on their beds and then knock on the doors and tell them to leave. Over time with plenty of praise, you can make it more difficult and more realistic by doing it in the dark. If they get it wrong or make a mistake, never tell them off or get angry, just point out where they could do better. For example, tell them not to bother collecting their favourite teddy bear next time, or going to the hall cupboard to collect a coat.

When they are a little older, you could try getting them to take a turn as the leader, where in consultation with Mum or Dad they choose where the 'fire' has been discovered and so define the safe escape route.

As long as you remain calm, don't pressurise the children, don't scare them, give them a lot of praise and support for 'winning' and being clever there shouldn't be a problem. You know your children so only you can decide how far you want to go with the exercises. Any practice evacuations you do arrange will pay off if there is an incident and you have to evacuate.

Key points
Some key points are:

- Evacuation awareness will prepare your child and family members for fire alarms and evacuations elsewhere. They will know that when the fire alarm sounds they should leave quietly, if it is at home, in the cinema, at the football stadium or sports hall.
- ALWAYS and I mean ALWAYS make sure that everyone involved knows when there is a practice evacuation. By doing that, they will automatically know that if nobody has planned a drill, any alarm and evacuation is the real thing. Having experienced the real thing, I know that there is an edge, a sense of purpose to a real evacuation, where practice evacuations generally tend to be a little too relaxed and complacent.
- Don't have a practice evacuation too often. The impact of the alarm will have reduced effect if too many practice evacuations are scheduled. When a small fire started in the workshop of an office block I was attending they sounded the alarm. Generally people looked at each other for a few minutes, then when the alarm wasn't turned off employees began to amble out of the building. The managing director had just started a sales presentation to a dozen potential clients, and he reacted to the clanging alarm bells by sending his secretary to turn the alarm off. She was sent to the third floor in the lift to see the building

supervisor and pass on the message from the MD. When she couldn't find him she went down to reception and was rather surprised to see firemen. The managing director's presentation was then quickly terminated when firemen told them they had to leave because there really was a fire. People must and should always react to an alarm as though it was real!

- With any evacuation, somebody should know, or have a very good idea how many people are in the building at any given time. They should act as leader, or fire marshal. They should attend the rally or meeting point outside with some sort of notebook or clipboard. As people evacuate the building they should report to the leader or fire marshal, so that he or she can make a note that they are out and any new information they can give. For example 'top floor clear, no sign of fire' or 'kitchen staff out but there is a fire in a chip pan'.

- When the fire brigade arrive at the scene, the fire marshal should be able to brief them on what has happened and give them any information on possible hazards. For example 'There were seven people in the building but they are all out. My husband says that he was doing some welding on his old motorbike and a fire has started. There are welding gas cylinders in the garage, a motorbike with a full fuel tank and a two gallon can of spare petrol.'

- The fire marshal should also make notes on how the evacuation went. It is vital that these notes are reviewed and acted on after the practice. For example, if nobody could find the key to the back door and the meeting point was underneath three feet of floodwater, you have to review and change your plans. In this example you should find out where the back door key went and why it wasn't where it should be, then make sure that in future it is always where it should be, or that there is a spare key permanently ready for an emergency. Take another look at the meeting place: if it is subject to flooding in heavy rain, select a new meeting place that will be dry.

- Practice the evacuation procedures too. For example:
  - ➤ Keep low. Smoke and heat rise, so in a fire, the air will be clearer lower down. Smoke coming from burning plastics can be highly toxic. Find and use the cleanest air supply you can, even if you have to crawl along the floor towards the exit.
  - ➤ If possible, and without delaying your exit from the building, consider covering your mouth and nose with a wet towel or sheet, that should help to protect your face and to filter out some of the smoke and fumes when you breathe.
  - ➤ Try to protect young children. In a real fire make sure that they have not become scared and hidden from the smoke and flames under the bed or in a wardrobe. Don't assume they have left, look for them.
  - ➤ Where at all possible cover all exposed skin with natural materials, for

53

example a woollen blanket or a folded sheet. Don't use man-made materials unless that is all that is available. The heat inside a building that is on fire can build up very quickly, and you will suffer more serious burns if a nylon sheet melts onto your skin. A damp woollen blanket offers considerable protection.

➢ Always make sure that you have some footwear available. Remember, when evacuating a burning building you may be walking through red hot cinders or broken glass while still inside the building. Slip-on shoes with a solid sole are ideal; avoid fluffy nylon slippers that could catch fire, or shoes that may take some while to put on!

➢ When you approach a door in a burning building, feel the door with the back of your hand. If the door feels hot there may be an inferno on the other side. You will feel heat through almost any door, including a wooden one. If the door feels OK, carefully touch the handle with the back of your hand. (The natural human reaction when touching something hot is for the hand to close and grasp the object. If you use your fingers to touch test a door or door handle and it is hot, your natural reaction could make you grab and hold that red hot handle. If you use the back of the hand, the natural reaction will be to close your fingers and pull safely away from the door handle.) If the door is hot and the handle is red hot, assume there is a serious fire on the other side of the door, especially if there is secondary evidence, such as smoke and flames coming under and around the door. If that is the case, find another exit route.

Torches

In case of a fire (or power cuts) a torch will be handy. I suggest that people keep a torch with working batteries beside their bed, so that if they do need one, they have it to hand and are so familiar with it that they can even reach out and get it through thick smoke.

Windows

The best and safest escape route is through a door. If you are upstairs, the best route is down the stairs and out of a door. If the stairs were blocked by fire, a window might be your only escape route. Be warned, although current regulations require that double glazing units should open fully to allow residents to escape through windows on upper floors, those regulations are quite new. Check to make sure that all upper storey windows will open fully, should they need to be used as an escape route.

Doors

Though security is our primary consideration, remember that in an emergency you may want to leave the property very quickly. I have advised you not to leave keys in locks for security purposes, but at night the rules change a little. If a fire starts at night, it will be dark, it will be smoky, you will be half asleep, disoriented and scared. If there is a fire, you don't want to have to hunt around the kitchen trying to guess where whoever locked up last night has put the key. The front and back doors are fire exits, make sure that they can be used quickly and easily. At night I would advise you to leave door chains off and consider leaving the key in the lock, or very close nearby to allow you and your family or guests to open doors at short notice.

Flood
Flooding is a hazard that more British families are facing. While you are reviewing your security, if you have any doubts as to your vulnerability to flooding you should make a note to check with the local authority and the company that supplies water locally. They can usually tell you if your house is susceptible to flooding. If you are performing a security check on a house you are thinking of buying, it is even more important. Insurance companies are likely to refuse to insure a property where there is a history of flooding or where flooding is likely. On the environment agency website www.environment-agency.gov.uk, you can type in a postcode and check flooding maps, which will give you a good idea of the risk of flooding for any given location and property.

Front door
The front door is important because it is usually the access point that faces the world and the access point that is used most. As you enter, check the quality and strength of the door.

Keys hidden outside
Most people have experienced the annoyance of being locked out of their own home for one reason or another. It is very easy to do, popping out to get something from the car and finding that the wind has blown the door shut. Alternately you may have had the annoying doorstep conversation with your partner when you get home from shopping that has you both saying 'But I thought you had the door keys'.

To avoid this problem many people are tempted to hide a door key somewhere outside the house. Don't do it. Criminals know that many people do that, especially where there are children in the family.

People used to leave a door key fastened inside the door on a length of string. To get in all you had to do was fish through the letter box, pull the string out and use the key tied to the end to open the door. That 'clever' trick got to be as well known as leaving a key under the front doormat so people stopped doing it.

Hiding keys in or under a flowerpot, bricks and gnomes won't fool a criminal either. I have even seen adverts for 'secure' key hiding places made to look like cobblestones, gnomes or other garden clutter. To my mind anyone who uses one of these plastic containers which are 'cleverly disguised' as something or other is recklessly stupid. Why spend a lot of time and money making your house safe and secure, then break your own security by leaving a key out for the criminals? No matter how clever your hiding place is, it will be discovered.

If you were a criminal watching a target house for a few days and saw a child come home, move a brick near the garage door, open the front door then return to that brick, how long would it take you to guess where a hidden key might be? Do you think that criminals don't read the newspapers? They will have seen the adverts for disguised key stores in the shape of garden frog, cobbles and logs and will have made it their business to know what they look like, because finding a key makes it a lot easier for them to get into your house.

Spare keys – countermeasures

✔ **Don't hide keys outside.**

✔ If you have to have an emergency key, give one each to two relatives or very close friends who live nearby. Why two? One of them might be out when you need your emergency key!

✔ Make sure that you trust your keyholders and anyone who lives with them! Uncle Bob may be thoroughly trustworthy, and Mrs Biggin from number 42 may be a wonderful lady, but who else is coming and going in that house? Uncle Bob's alcoholic son, or the new drug addict boyfriend of Mrs Biggin's lovely daughter may not be as trustworthy!

Softwood door

Many wooden doors are cheaply made and have little strength; one kick will break them open. By swinging the door shut you will feel the weight of the door. Grasp the door on the edge opposite the hinges, one hand near the top and the other as low as is comfortable. Then try to twist the door (gently pull with the right hand and push with the left. A softwood door will often flex showing how little strength there is in it. A cheap door feels light, and you can easily mark the wood by gouging at it with a thumbnail (do it on the edge just above a hinge where it will not be seen). This softwood has little strength and is very susceptible to rot and decay as well. Kicking it will splinter the door and often the frame too. (Don't do it to test it, just be aware that a softwood door offers little strength.)

Door panels
You should be aware that the design of some less expensive doors could include a weakness that is well known. Where a door includes panels set into the door, the panels sometimes have very little strength. At worst the panels may be thin plywood, and only let into the frame in a shallow groove, so that one good kick often makes the door panel fall inwards. The criminal has the option of crawling in through the hole he has made, or reaching inside to release the lock to open the door. A flimsy door panel doesn't even make much noise when it is smashed!

Hardwood Door
A hardwood door is actually hard, and gouging it with a thumbnail will break the nail rather than the door. Swinging it back and forth you will be able to feel the weight. Trying to twist it is usually futile, they are so rigid that there will be little movement, but you are welcome to try. Remember that no matter how strong the door, if the frame, hinges and locks are cheap or badly installed, you will reduce the protection that the hardwood door provides.

UPVC (double glazed)
UPVC (plastic) double glazed doors seem quite secure because of the standard multiple point locking mechanisms built into the door, but many of them suffer from panel weakness. As with wooden doors, the door panels are particularly vulnerable – one kick or a blow with a weight will smash the panel out, leaving a nice access point, or at least free access to reach in and open what's left of the door from the inside! Newer and more expensive doors have steel frames built into the carcass of the door, which combined with the multiple locking point mechanisms do make them very secure, but they are not widely used and rarely found in older doors.

Door frame
Remember to check the quality and fixing of the door frame. If the frame is weak and badly fitted it will give way and the strength of the door is irrelevant. Weakness can be found for a number of reasons, such as:

• The frame is constructed of cheap wood or is rotten.
• The frame is secured with the wrong fittings or not enough fittings were used.
• The structure of the wall to which the frame is secured is substandard.
• The frame is the wrong size for the opening it has been used in.

57

You should test the security and strength of the frame. Grasp the frame firmly and try to move it. If there is any movement re-fix it to make sure it can withstand attempts to gain access.

Locks

No matter how strong the door is, it has one fundamental flaw and that is that doors are designed and built to swing open easily. Their function is to give easy access to people and that makes them vulnerable. They have to open easily, but they should also be easy to shut and secure when required and that is achieved by fitting locks and bolts to the door. The effectiveness of the security of any door depends on the quality, number, fixing and placement of locks and bolts.

A night latch is convenient because it secures the door and the owner only needs to carry a small key to allow them to open and close the lock. The night latch

Night latch

Mortice lock and catch
plate

usually screws to the surface of the door so offers minimal protection against physical assault. As a single point fastening the night latch offers poor protection because one solid kick will break the door open. A two-point locking scheme offers better protection, especially if it uses what is called a five lever mortice deadlock and even better if it is to British Standard BS3621.

Locks and fittings are available from good hardware stores. Those illustrated are shown courtesy of Screwfix, a large company which sells locks, tools and materials (www.screwfix.com).

A mortice lock is a stronger fixing method because it is installed inside the door. A suitable slot has to be cut into the edge of the door, and the lock is buried within the wood where it becomes part of the structure of the door. Holes are cut through to accommodate the handle and key slot, which allow the lock to be operated. As with most locks a catch plate is secured into the doorframe, reinforcing the point where the mortice bolt engages the frame.

Different locksmiths give different advice as to the type, location and fixing of door locks. Technically, the advice will differ depending on a number of factors. For example, considerations that will be taken into account when proposing adequate protection for a door will include the following:

- The **premises** in question and **what they hold**. For example, a paper bag storeroom will require less protection than an electronic goods storeroom.
- **Access** to the door. If it is only open to pedestrian access the threat is reduced, but if it is open to vehicular access a secure locking scheme may include strategically placed anti-vehicle bollards.
- **Length of time the door will be exposed to a threat**. If a night patrol checks the door every 15 minutes, the maximum exposure time of that door to a threat will be 15 minutes.
- The **material** used in the construction of the door. Softwood doors are not as strong as hardwood doors. A UPVC door is not as strong as a hardwood door with a steel skin on both sides.
- **Skills and experience** used to **install** the door. A strong door badly sited and installed is of questionable value. If a tradesperson installs a door, securing the frame into the surrounding masonry, the door and frame take on the strength of the surrounding wall.
- Design and presence of **windows**. Some doors are designed to allow ventilation and so are fitted with louvers, and it is easy for a criminal to cut or break through a series of louvers to gain access. Similarly, the presence of glass in a door reduces its effectiveness as a security barrier. A door that has a window beside it is as secure as the window! It is pointless fitting the world's strongest door if any lout with a brick can break the window to get in!

French windows and patio doors

French windows are probably the most vulnerable door in any property. They are usually located at the back of the premises, so a criminal can work on them unobserved and uninterrupted. The doors are designed to let in light and be easily opened wide to give access to the garden on a warm dry day and as such are designed more for looks and wide access than solid security.

Patio doors are often newer and of a better build and design quality, but they are still vulnerable to a criminal who manages to get to the back of the premises.

Both types of doors can easily be levered open with simple tools, unless the owner has taken steps to secure them.

Door security – countermeasures

As a general rule for best effect I would suggest the following:

✔ Buy the best door you can afford and can justify for the use you have in mind.

✔ Have the door installed by a skilled tradesperson.

✔ Ensure that the frame is of equal quality and that it is firmly and correctly secured to the surrounding masonry.

✔ Use the best hinges suitable for the application.

✔ Install hinge bolts – bolts that fit into the hinge edge of the door and reinforce the strength of the door on the hinge side. Expensive locks are a waste of money if a criminal can simply kick the door off the hinges on the hinge side.

✔ Use at least a two-point fastening scheme. Your locksmith will advise you where to fit the locks, but generally it is advised that one lock is fitted approximately two fifths of the way down from the top of the door and another just under halfway up from the bottom. At least one lock should be a properly installed mortice lock.

✔ When you have gone to the trouble of installing such a secure door, lock it when you go out.

✔ For safety reasons DON'T leave the mortice lock locked when you are in the house, particularly at night, in case you need to get out of the house in a hurry. Use the night latch!

✔ Pay particular attention to the survey of French windows and patio doors. As a priority get the locks, hinges, tracks and security of all French windows and patio doors checked by an expert if you have any doubts as to their security and strength.

Other door furniture

Depending on their use, doors may need other fixtures and fittings, which are collectively known as 'door furniture'. For example:

Letterbox
A letterbox makes a door vulnerable. Cutting the hole weakens the structure of the door. Criminals have been known to use long poles to fish through a letterbox to remove car keys and valuables from the hall of a residence. Garage letterboxes and car-key drop off bins have been raided by criminals who drive away in hire cars

that have been returned out of hours, or cars that have been left at a garage for services.

If required a letterbox should be fitted by a professional. Door manufacturers often recommend locations for letterbox slots for specific door designs. If they do, take their advice, but remember that a letterbox should:

- be large enough to accommodate postal deliveries
- be conveniently situated – the postman or woman will not be happy to bend to use a letterbox at the bottom of a door
- be fitted with an appropriate external flap and internal draft guard, to avoid wasting heat in the house
- possibly be fitted with a wire cage to catch mail and prevent foreign material being pushed through (there should be a smoke detector in the hall – it is not unknown for brainless louts to push fireworks through letterboxes).

Window bars
In some circumstances, where glass windows are fitted to a door or beside doors, fitting window bars or grilles provides an added deterrent and an extra measure of security. See 'Windows' below.

Door viewer/spy hole
Where a solid door is fitted, you may wish to install a viewer, which allows you to see who is outside the door. The viewers are usually fitted with a wide-angle lens on the outside, which presents you with a view of everything outside your door, allowing you to decide whether it is safe to open the door or not.

Weather strip
Not really a security item but included because many doors need them. It is fitted to the bottom on the outside of the door and it is designed to prevent water from running down the face of the door and running inside under the door. A weather strip will also help to prevent rot on the door, and avoid water penetration and swelling of the wood.

Hinge bolts
These bolts reinforce the hinge side of the door. They are fitted at intervals along the hinge edge of the door, I usually advise fitting at least three. They are quite easy to fit. Drill a hole on the centre line of the hinge edge of the door to an appropriate size and depth as per the installation instructions, then screw the bolts home. When all bolts have been fitted, I gently close the door until the hinge bolts touch the doorframe. Applying gentle pressure, without straining the hinges, you

61

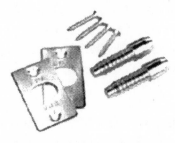

Hinge bolts and catch plates

can easily mark the frame where the hinge bolts will engage. Drill a hole for the bolt, mark out and cut a rebate for the catch plates then screw them in and the job is done. When hinge bolts are fitted, a door cannot be kicked off its hinges without totally destroying the door, and if that much force is used, nothing will protect the property.

Internal door furniture

Other door furniture can be used inside the door, some of which is primarily used to increase security while some have secondary security benefits. For example:

Mail basket
A metal basket fastened to the inside of the letterbox will catch mail that is posted through the door. The primary purpose is to collect the mail, keep it tidy, prevent it being caught under the door and possibly being damaged when the door is opened and finally, making it convenient to collect incoming mail rather than scrabbling around on the floor for it. The secondary security benefit is that a basket prevents or hampers access through the letterbox, so criminals cannot hook car and door keys off hall tables. (Make sure that no keys are available or visible through your letterbox anyway.)

Letterbox covers
Positioned inside a letterbox they will at least stop draughts and can prevent rodents and insects from entering through a letterbox, especially if it is fitted to the bottom of a door. If they are spring-loaded they can stop or at least hinder visibility and access if a criminal does try to hook car keys or anything else through the letterbox.

Draft excluders
The presence of draft excluders shows that the property owner has taken steps to make the house as comfortable as they can, but as a security consideration *they ring an alarm bell to me*. The need for draft excluders indicates to me that the door is poorly fitted or poorly maintained and so is evidently a potential weak point, open to attack. Draft excluders make me look further at the strength, fitting, quality and security of a door.

Weather strip
Similar to the draft excluders, additional weather stripping indicates to me that the door is not as sound or well fitted as it could and should be. Weather strips tell me to look closer at the door and consider replacement!

Door viewer/spy hole
If a door viewer/spy hole is fitted – try it. See what you can see from inside the door. Get some help, ask somebody to hide to the right or left of the door, and see if you can still see them using the wide angle lens on the outside of the door. This will tell you if there are any places where a potential attacker could hide and not be seen using the viewer. Late at night if there is a knock at the door, and all you can see is what appears to be an old lady asking to use the phone because her car has broken down, is it safe? Could a burly robber be standing two feet to the right or just out of sight in the alcove on the doorstep? Check now to be sure. Identify any blind spots at your leisure and remove them now! For example, if you find that a criminal could be hiding to the left of the doorstep, put a trellis there, if somebody does hide there you will have time to slam the door before they can get around the trellis and thorny trailing rose you plant there. If criminals could hide in the shadows of the alcove on the doorstep, fit a light which you can turn on and off from inside the door so that they have no shadows to hide in.

Door chains
Door chains can be fitted to allow a door to be opened a little way to see who is there, without giving easy access to criminals who might be outside. Because the chain is short and engaged in the locking mechanism, it can only be removed when the door is shut, giving the resident an opportunity to lock the door and call the police if they are worried that a caller presents a threat. There are many different types of door chains, but they all have the same limitations. They have to be fitted properly, and they only work if they are used. It is pointless having a door chain fitted if you do not attach it before opening the door. If you have one – use it.

Remember, a door chain should ONLY be used to check to see who is at the door. Ordinarily it should not be engaged. They usually have some sort of hook that will let you hook the chain safely and tidily out of the way. With the chain in the safety, storage position if there is a fire or other crisis, you can get out of the door easily without fumbling to take off a security door chain.

Notices and signs
Notices and signs can be a deterrent, and so can help to increase security and prevent nuisance. Signs such as 'We do not buy from doorstep salesmen', 'No free

63

newspapers or circulars', 'Door Alarmed', or 'CCTV In Use' can deter unwanted callers.

Notes

Notes can be an invitation to a criminal. Leaving a note stuck to the front door saying 'Gone out – deliveries to number 42' is a Christmas present to a criminal. Writing and leaving that sort of note tells the criminal that your house is empty and unattended. Worse, if number 42 is several houses away, that probably means that the neighbouring houses are empty too or they would have taken the delivery.

Similarly, leave a nice friendly and quite common note for the milkman saying 'On holiday, no milk until Saturday 27th', and you may as well leave your valuables in the street. Think security!

Top and bottom locks

Additional security can be obtained by fitting sliding bolts or security rack bolts to the inside of the door at the top and bottom. These additional fixings make it a lot harder to break down a door, but I question their value if the door is already fitted with hinge bolts and a two-point locking system. Additional bolts undoubtedly make the door more secure, but they cause me some concern. Firstly they can only be used from the inside, which means they can only be used when you are in the house when the house is a lot less likely to be a target for criminals.

More importantly, if top and bottom bolts are secured at night they are a potentially fatal barrier to your quick escape if there is a fire! Under normal circumstances an adult can easily slide back a top and bottom bolt to open the door, but what about unusual circumstances such as the confused panic of a house fire at night? What if there is a child in the house and the adult has already been overcome by smoke, could the child reach the top bolt? What if the adult is partially overcome with smoke, would those bolts be so easy to release if you were in a state of collapse? Bolts do increase security, but I always advise people to think long and hard before fitting and using them.

Windows

Glass used in and beside doors can be used to make the hall lighter, to see who is at the door, or for decorative purposes. Standard glass is fragile, and as such is a security risk. Apart from the threat of injury to children running up to the door or tripping and falling down stairs into the glass, windows are a security threat. It is far too easy to break glass to gain access. Wherever possible I advise against installing doors with glass panels, and given the choice would prefer not to have windows beside doors. After all, why install a really solid and expensive security door, when the window next to it can be removed with half a brick or an automatic centre punch? (An automatic centre punch is something used by engineers. It makes a small dent in metal at the point you want to drill a hole. Unfortunately criminals use them because they are easy to obtain, pocket sized and easy to hide, and used on a house or car window, they easily and fairly quietly break glass.) If at all possible avoid having glass in or beside a door.

Windows – countermeasures

✔ Avoid glass in doors and beside doors.
✔ If glass is present, consider replacing the door and possibly replacing the side windows with more solid options.
✔ If you need to retain the windows in or beside a door, consider fitting metal grills over them to make them more secure. (Remember that a landlord may have objections to any of this work and with listed buildings it may be a planning permission problem.)

Entrance hall

You should now start reviewing each room, paying first attention to the access points to the room. The entrance hall is unique in as much as you have considered the front door and any alarm system separately.

You should now be looking at the hall with security in mind.

Keys
Make a note of any keys you can see, and check those notes when you reach the keys section below.

Lighting
An entrance hall should have bright lighting, and if possible a switch that operates an external porch light to help you see who is at the door. The brighter the light you install, the more exposed a criminal will be and the less likely he is to target your house. If you go to switch on the external porch light and find it doesn't work, assume that there is a criminal on your doorstep! It is of course possible that your visitor is innocent and the bulb has simply failed, but it is also possible that they removed the bulb so that you couldn't see and identify them. Be cautious and be safe.

Letter box

Check the location and quality of the letterbox. If it is located at waist level, it is ideally placed for a criminal to look through to see what is inside, even if they don't bother to push a stick through with a hook on the end to take your car keys off the hall table. An internal draught excluder in the form of a top and bottom brush will prevent easy viewing and make it more difficult to 'fish' things through the letterbox; an internal flap is even better – especially if combined with the brush draft excluders, and possibly with a mail basket.

Indications

I have in the past advised elderly people to 'dress' their hall, as in 'stage dressing'. Let us assume that we are in the hall of an old lady who lives alone. A visitor can see a lady's coat, a lady's umbrella, a headscarf and maybe a pair of an older woman's walking shoes. Remember that a criminal will be looking for and reading the clues, and in this case all he sees are clues that point to a frail old lady living alone. I advise the family of elderly people who live alone to help them to dress their hall, to introduce some evidence of other occupants. For example, a strong used dog lead on a side table hints that there is a large dog around somewhere. A pair of men's walking boots left in the hall with a man's jacket and baseball cap indicate to a caller with less than good intentions that there may be a younger man around somewhere or due back soon!

I have seen a large pair of men's running shoes casually tossed under the stairs in plain view of the front door in the hall of a 96-year-old woman, hinting at the presence of a big and athletic man.

The entrance hall is or should be as far as strangers will get into your house, especially with the door chain fitted and used, so anything you can do to make it secure and put off a criminal the better. What could you dress your hall with to indicate that the house and resident is not an easy target? If you are elderly, ask younger relatives to donate some items, or even visit the local charity shop for some appropriate items to leave on view!

Alarm system

If there is an alarm system fitted, the control panel is usually near to the front door in the entrance hall, and sometimes incorporates one or two panic buttons around the house that the householder can hit to instantly activate the alarm bells.

Questions you should be asking about alarms are:

- If there is an alarm system, check it. Is it working? How often has it been triggered, and what triggered it? A badly adjusted alarm may be set at a sensitivity level that will not go off even if an intruder holds a party in your lounge, or may be so sensitive that it is triggered a dozen times each night by passing moths!

- What points of access are covered by the alarm and by what method? (Contact breaker, pressure pads, movement sensors, heat sensors, light beams, noise sensors, etc.) Are any access points not covered? For example, a new patio door installed after the alarm was installed may not be alarmed! (Of course the owner of a house you are thinking of buying won't give you this information because that would be a security breach.)
- Is the burglar alarm system monitored by the company who supplied it, or does it rely on neighbours and people passing by to call the police?
- Are there any panic buttons? If so, where are they located?
- How often is the alarm used – that is, turned on rather than left off? A lot of people can't be bothered to spend a few minutes setting an alarm, so they have it installed and rarely use it.
- Who has the combination, key or code to turn the alarm off or on? Remember that previous tenants had the code, cleaners, builders and other workers may have been given it. Children are often careless in the use of a code, and forget to shield their hands when keying a number in when a stranger is present. If in doubt, change the number and then restrict the number of people who have that number or code.
- Does the system have a record of activating for no apparent reason?

Alarm – countermeasures

- ✔ An alarm system that is never used is not worth having.
- ✔ An alarm system that goes off too often will be ignored by everyone.
- ✔ An alarm system that does not cover all access points is not worth having.
- ✔ Remember, if the alarm sounds, there is a reason. Use extreme caution when checking the premises. If there are any signs of criminal activity, such as broken glass or open doors, call the police and ask them to check the premises for intruders.
- ✔ If the alarm sounds and you disturb an intruder, make as much noise as you can to scare them away. They will want to escape, and you don't want to try any heroics that may leave you seriously injured, paralysed or dead.
- ✔ A dummy alarm box will put off opportunists, but it will not fool a career criminal.
- ✔ Beware of the return visit! It has been known for a criminal to trigger an alarm deliberately, then retire to watch the activity. The premises are checked for intruders and found to be empty, they reset the alarm and go away. The criminal then triggers the alarm again and hides away to watch. After one or two alarms, the key holder usually assumes that there is a fault in the system, so they

67

do not bother resetting the alarm and make a note to call the alarm engineer in the morning. The criminal returns and tests the system by trying to trigger the alarm again, if it does not go off he knows he has a clear field to take what he wants with no alarm to cause problems.

Telephone access and locations

Check for telephone access and the location of phone cables and plugs. Often the phone line enters through the entrance hall and then feeds to any other phones in the house. Having a phone in the bedroom allows you to summon assistance if you think there is a fire or an intruder downstairs; without it you will have to come downstairs to risk the potential threat to summon assistance. The widespread use and availability of mobile phones can do away with the need for a phone in the bedroom, as long as they are not left on charge in the kitchen at night!

Ground floor rooms

You should now check all ground floor rooms in order. With your back to the front door, follow the wall to your left, turning into rooms on the left and following the wall around that room until you exit and continue the tour, eventually returning to the front door. Don't forget to look into all cupboards, store rooms and wardrobes etc.

In each room pay particular attention to doors, windows and skylights in external walls and ceilings because that is where intruders might find access.

Ground floor windows

For all ground floor windows, check to see if the window is closed and locked. Are window locks fitted? Is the key to any window lock in the lock or removed and held in a safe place? Check the fit of the window – is it loose, does it rattle? Is there sign of rot in a wooden frame? Just as we checked the quality and fit of the front door we have to check each window to see if it will keep intruders out. While you are there take the opportunity to review the level of maintenance of the windows – will they keep the cold and weather out as well?

At night I advise you to leave bedroom windows unlocked, or perhaps leave the window lock keys in upstairs windows when you are in the house. If there is a fire, you want to be able to escape quickly and easily. If the window is locked and the key is in the kitchen you could be trapped.

Unlock and open the window, and check to see how easily it operates. Check to see how easy it is to shut and lock. If the window is stiff and the lock is temperamental you may be tempted to leave the window insecure if you have to leave in a hurry. Windows and doors should operate easily, and be easy to shut, lock and unlock.

Note any problems with maintenance, installation, fit, operation and locks, and make sure that problems are attended to as soon as is practicable.

Ground floor doors

As with the front door and ground floor windows, patio doors, back doors, french windows and any other doors on the ground floor are most vulnerable to attack. Remember that criminals prefer to use doors. Using a door makes it easier to get in and out. If they are seen, somebody using a door isn't anywhere near as suspicious as somebody climbing in or out of a broken window. Make the same checks for fit, strength, operation and locks as you did with the front door, note any problems and resolve them as soon as you can.

Basements

When you have finished checking the ground floor, if there is a basement or cellar, go down and check it now. With your back to the stairs, follow the left wall and tour the basement or cellar. Pay particular attention to access points, coal delivery chutes, windows and doors. As with all doors and windows, check them thoroughly. Remember that any external stair well with steps down to the basement will be ideal for a criminal, because they can slip down the access steps and work on a basement door or window unseen, giving them plenty of time to break in.

Upper floor doors

When any basement and ground floor checks are finished, work your way up and around each upper floor again following the left wall (which should make sure you don't miss any rooms). Check all windows and doors, paying particular attention to doors and windows that open onto a flat roof, a balcony or anywhere an intruder may have easy access.

In multiple occupancy buildings a balcony or flat roof that gives access to another flat or room is particularly vulnerable. These doors and windows should be treated the same and be made as secure as the front door to any property. If they are hidden from passing traffic or pedestrians they should be made even more secure than a front door while still allowing for escape in a fire.

Where there is a balcony, you will have surveyed it in your close perimeter **69** survey, but it is worth checking for access routes and hand and foot holds from above, below and to the side. Note any problems and take action to resolve them.

Loft/loft conversions

If the loft has been converted into accommodation you will check it when you work your way up to that floor level. However, even if the loft is not converted you should check the storage space in the roof. In an old terrace I surveyed, I found that the dividing wall was incomplete. There was a gap large enough for me to climb through the roof spaces of the whole row of houses, giving easy access down into each of the houses in the terrace from their lofts.

Be careful. Most lofts are not boarded – that is, there is no floor! The roof timbers of the top floor have plasterboard attached to the underside to make a ceiling for the top floor rooms. In the loft the top of those rafters is not covered with floorboards. You can only move around in the loft by using the rafters as rungs or stepping-stones to walk on. Between the rafters there will only be a thin layer of plaster between you and the room below so don't stand on it. If in doubt or unsure, do your survey from the ladder using a torch and standing in the loft access, without actually climbing into the loft.

Check the end walls, especially if you are in a terrace or other property that shares a common wall or walls. With a party wall, there is a risk of unwanted access but there is also a fire risk. If the property next door catches fire and the party wall is incomplete the fire will travel through to your property, and if undetected could burn your house down as well, or at least seriously damage it.

While you are in the loft area do your maintenance checks as well. Check for signs of water ingress, damp patches, woodworm or other infestations to the fabric of the building as well as wasp nests. Check the quality of any water tanks and pipe work. You don't have to be an expert plumber to do this, just look for the obvious. Is there a lid on any water tank? Can you see any signs of stains or white scale around joints and connections that may indicate leaks? Are the tanks and pipes lagged to prevent them freezing in cold weather?

Make a note of anything that causes you concern and get an expert in to check it and correct it as soon as possible. With house maintenance, ignoring a problem is not an acceptable option! If you ignore a problem you will eventually have to pay to resolve it and it will cause you a lot more trouble and cost you a lot more to fix the longer you leave it. If you are thinking of selling your house, potential buyers will find structural problems and either refuse to buy it or offer a reduced price because of the defects.

Some houses have windows set into the gable end of the roof, and some have windows set into the roof itself. If so, check their quality, repair and security.

House Survey – Keys

Take a moment to consider the following question. Sit and think about it for a while, then write down what you think the answer is. How many sets of keys are there to your house and who holds them? Don't read any further until you have done that, then with your list finished read on!

So how many sets of keys do you think are in circulation? Now, how many sets of keys *could* be in circulation?

When a house is sold, one or two sets of keys are surrendered and passed on to the new owner, but most families have more than two sets of keys. That means that anyone who used to own your house could still have keys that they kept for sentimental reasons (our first house)! They may be thrown in a box at the back of their garage with a nice brass tag showing the address they come from, but they exist somewhere!

Now widen the consideration. One or all of the previous owners may have given a forgotten set of keys to a relative for safe keeping, or given a key to the lady who used to clean for them. They may have forgotten that they gave the plumber a key the time he had to replace the boiler when they were on holiday. That nice Mrs Biggins who used to live over the road had a key, because she used to pop in at lunchtime to let their dog out. Oh yes, the man at number 73 used to service the car, so he had a garage key! Come to think about it little Jason lost his keys at school three times so we gave him a new set each time! Then of course there are the six or seven estate agencies, over the past 15 years they all had a set of keys when they were trying to sell the house and they may have taken copies!

So, how many sets of keys did you write down on your list? Now that you have read the information above, how many more sets or individual keys do you think you could or should add to that list?

There is no point at all in improving the security of your home when you don't know, or are not certain who has or may have a set of keys to the property. If you have no control over the keys, you have no control over the security and safety of the premises. If you haven't changed the locks since you moved in, any number of people you don't know and have never met may have keys to your house! Remember previous owners may not have been as security conscious or careful in their control of keys as you will hopefully be!

Even if you are careful when making duplicates and giving sets of keys to people, how careful are you with your keys? You may think that they are safe on a hook in the kitchen or in a little bowl in the hall, but they may not be. Dishonest window cleaners have snatched sets of keys, had copies cut and then returned the originals when they came in to rinse a sponge, or they might just declare that the keys were found in the drive! That copied key with a list of the valuables the window cleaner has spotted in the house could be sold off to a burglar or used by the window cleaner in his night job as a thief! Keys in the hallway could be taken by somebody coming in to deliver a parcel, read the electricity meter or measure up for new carpets.

Even leaving keys in the hall could be a risk, because thieves have found that fishing through the letterbox with a cane with a hook on the end can be quite rewarding. While you are in bed, it's worth a criminal investing 15 minutes of his time fishing through the letterbox, if the reward is that he gets the keys to your BMW or Porsche. All keys should be out of sight and out of reach of the door and any visitors who are passing through.

Keys – countermeasures

✔ Locks give you security, keys give you access. Remember that unless you are very careful with your keys, you might as well not bother installing locks and locking things up in the first place.

✔ Never leave any keys unattended – for example, in your car ignition while you go to open the garage or in your bag while you nip to the toilet. (Your bag will almost certainly also have something showing your address, so the thief will have your keys AND your address.)

✔ Never leave keys inside windows, on desks at work, in your car – in fact anywhere that they may be taken or copied.

✔ Be wary of labelling keys – you don't want to tell a thief or any dishonest person who finds your lost keys where your house is or what the car number is.

✔ If you want to put a label on keys, make it your mobile phone number. If you lose your keys and somebody calls, DON'T give your address, ask them to meet you at a convenient public place like the library or supermarket. Remember that they could be honest citizens just wanting to give you your keys back so don't be too harsh on them. Agree to meet at a mutually convenient public place. Take the keys back, but on the basis of your opinion of the person who hands them back to you, consider changing all the locks anyway. For example, if you just don't like the look or sound of him he may be a criminal, so trust your instinct and change the locks.

✔ Always make sure you know how many keys you have cut for any given lock. Always record who has what key, then you know who has access, and know who to contact if you need a spare or have to replace the lock and issue new keys.

✔ Before issuing a key to anyone, decide whether they really need a key of their own. Is it just for their convenience? If so they can wait to be let in by somebody else! Do they really need unattended access of their own? Do you want them to have unattended access of their own?

✔ How many keys do people carry? Most people have or carry at least a few mystery keys – they can't actually remember what they fit. When you change jobs or move, get rid of old keys. Spring clean your key ring today. Make a note of the keys you carry. Decide if you really need to carry the key to the lawn mower, or the key to your first motorbike that you keep as a keepsake. Remove any keys from your keyring if you don't need to carry or don't know what they are. Any that you recognise but no longer need – discard. Any you don't need to carry (like the lawnmower key) put somewhere safe like a kitchen drawer. Any keys you don't want, don't use and can't remember what they are, put in a sealed envelope in the back of a kitchen drawer marked 'Unknown Keys' with today's date. A year from now if you still don't remember what they are, and haven't needed them – discard them.

✔ Never allow strangers to have unattended access anywhere that keys are kept. It is too easy to take a key.

✔ Make sure that everyone keeps their keys safe – put them on a chain, or on a clip inside a handbag or case. That way they shouldn't be forgotten, because people know they always unclip the keys, use them then clip them straight back into the handbag, etc.

✔ Avoid using key racks which are helpfully labelled 'BMW, Garage, Speedboat', etc.

✔ If you find that a key doesn't fit any more, change the locks. It is not unknown for criminals to simply switch keys, it takes a second or two and the loss may not be noticed for days or weeks. It works like this: the criminal takes a door key and substitutes one that looks the same. The key owner still thinks they have the five keys they always carry including a back door key! Because they never use that key, they have no idea that the key that they think is their back door key has been replaced by a similar key. (A reminder that if you don't need to carry the key – don't carry it.) Meanwhile the criminal is at large for weeks with a key to the back door of your house or worse still the key to the back door to your shop!

✔ If you have lost a key, or have taken over a property and don't know what keys are in circulation, there is only one remedy and that is to change all of the locks. With new locks, you have total control over who has a key to your house, garage or shed. You will issue a new key to anyone you think *needs* access to the house.

✔ When managing keys, keep the number of keys to a minimum.

✔ Review your list of key holders. If circumstances change you may be able to, or have to ask for keys to be returned. If so, update your list, and consider changing the locks anyway.

✔ For extra security you can buy a security lock, which means that keys can only be cut at specialist security stores, they cannot be copied at any shoe repair shop or market stall.

✔ Seriously consider issuing a single key and not sets of keys. For example, if you have children who may lose their keys, only issue them with a single key to either the front or back door. (Given a choice select the door with the lock that is easiest and cheapest to replace.) Then if the children lose their key, only that single door has been compromised, which means you only have to replace that single lock. If the child loses a set of keys you may be regularly replacing every lock in the house!

✔ Are there any keys available to a criminal who sticks a cane with a hook on the end through the door? A lot of cars have been stolen with the owner's keys that have been fished out through the letterbox or a broken window. Move keys away from letterboxes – fit a mail basket, internal flap and brush draught excluder as well to prevent 'fishing'.

✔ If you have a cleaner or other employee, or a lodger, or any other non-family member of the household, I strongly suggest that you replace all of the locks to which they had a key when the relationship is terminated. If relationships break down and tenants are evicted, or employees sacked or a lover is dumped, they could all hold a grudge. Why risk them coming back with a duplicate key to leave the taps on, take the television or put rotten kippers under all of the seat cushions? Change the locks!

✔ Don't leave house keys in your car. If the car is broken into, the criminal has your house keys, could well have the full address from documents in the car, and from the state and quality of the car also has a fairly good idea of your wealth and possessions.

✔ If your keys were in your car, coat or briefcase or anything else that was stolen for that matter, change the locks.

✔ Never, ever give, loan or leave house keys with a builder or other workmen.

✔ I would never ever, leave keys in the tender care of estate agents or anyone else. The minute you hand a key over to an organisation rather than a person, you have totally and irrevocably breached your security.

House Survey – Valuable Contents

When doing a full house security survey on your own home, you should also do a valuable contents survey. (If you are performing a house security survey on a house you are thinking of buying, you clearly won't be doing a valuable contents survey.)

A valuable contents survey requires you to retrace your steps through all floors of the house starting at the front door. As you pass through each room you should note the valuable contents, particularly the sort of things that a criminal would be interested in taking. Remember to open every door to include contents of cupboards, wardrobes, trunks, etc. to include things that are not actually visible or on show, such as, Great Aunt Susan's jewellery, which is kept in the bottom of the wardrobe. Then there is the wedding gift of the antique vase, you think it is so ugly that you keep it in the airing cupboard or loft – and don't forget the digital camera in your sock drawer, etc.

Make a note of the things that need to be photographed as an addition to any serial numbers and descriptions that you write down. If at all possible, mark your postcode and house name or number on each item. An ultraviolet pen can be used for this, but items have to be marked in an area where handling or cleaning and polishing will not wear the marking away.

Every house in the country has a postcode, which identifies a small group of houses. The addition of your house number (or the first few letters of the house name) will identify your house. If any property then comes into the possession of the police, they can check the postcode and contact you to ask why the person they have in custody has your television! If you can say it was stolen last night, that is evidence, just as much as if you say you sold it through a newspaper advert to a Mr Smith!

An opportunistic burglar will take cash and small items that can easily be carried and can easily be resold, such as cameras, jewellery, personal stereos, MP3 music players, watches etc. Some burglars will be more organised and will arrive with transport, so they could take hi-fi systems, televisions, DVD players, computers etc. For a major country home containing antiques and artwork, it is not unheard of for criminals to bring a removal lorry and spend some time clearing hundreds of thousands of pounds' worth of property.

You will know what valuables could be targeted at your particular home. You should make a note of the contents of each room, describing where possible the following information:

- Item description (e.g. Flat Screen 38 inch television)
- Make (e.g. Panasonic)
- Item model (e.g. Model PS/345-2v)
- Serial number (e.g. P87-FS8650-7642-22)
- Unique marks (1 inch x-shaped scratch above on/off switch)
- Other information (for example a jewellery valuation and date given)
- Is a photograph needed?
- Is it marked with a postcode? If so where is it marked?

Photographs

Wherever possible take photographs of items that might be hard to describe, (for example, jewellery, antiques, ceramics, artwork etc.). When you take a photo, picture the object from front, rear and side views if it will help to identify it. Always include a size scale in the picture – a 12 inch ruler is best, but I have seen fifty pence coins used in photographs to indicate the size of jewellery. Make sure that you keep a copy of the printed picture on file, and keep the negatives or digital image safe.

If property is lost, photographs make it a lot easier for you to show the police what is missing. Even for something as simple as a bicycle, a photograph saves a lot of time. Try to describe your bike from memory, or a bike belonging to a relative. What is the frame size, style, colour? (Especially when manufacturers mix colours – try to tell the police your bike frame was fluorescent red, yellow and green, with the cross bar graduating from yellow at the saddle end, to green at the handlebars except for bands of black where the water bottle and puncture repair kit are fastened.) Where is the frame number, what is the frame number? Producing a colour picture of your bike, ride on mower, jewellery, etc. and saying to the police 'this is it', is a whole lot easier.

A photograph is even more important if jewellery and antiques are stolen, especially with a size scale in shot to show anyone how big the object is.

Video footage

Like still pictures, video can be used to show valuables. A tour of the house featuring key items is better than describing the contents of the home and can help people in a house with a lot of objects to identify and remember what is missing after a raid. A video image is not a substitute for records of make, model and serial number etc. The video tape will be additional information.

Insurance

A bonus of having video and photographs available is that it could help with insurance valuations after a fire or other disaster. Footage of the home with the valuables in place is better than showing an assessor a pile of rubble and assuring them that you really did have a Ming Dynasty vase, flat screen TV in every room, and priceless family heirlooms! Your claim is more likely to be accepted and processed quickly if you can give details. One insurance company reported that only 14% of claimants knew the make, model and serial number of the property they were claiming for.

Telling the criminals what you have

Do you advertise the fact when you buy new electronic goods? You don't think you do, but you might! Forget the computer on show in the conservatory window and the latest flat screen TV in the lounge. We aren't yet thinking about that nice laptop or electronic organiser carelessly left in the car. We're still considering the house, but more specifically what you throw out.

Everything is shipped and delivered in packages and as soon as we get it home we unpack and install it. It might be the latest hi-fi, a laptop computer or the latest flat screen televisions for the kitchen and the kids' bedrooms. Then we dump the box outside beside the bin and later put the box out for the dustman – and in doing so we also advertise to criminals that we just installed a brand new 'whatever-it-says-on-the-box'. The criminals know that, and they are clever enough to walk, cycle or drive round on rubbish collection day to see which house has thrown out some nice new and expensive looking boxes. It doesn't take Einstein to see that the people at number 42 have just unpacked and installed a wide screen television, top of the range computer or other deliciously tempting target.

Be careful and be green. Break the packaging down, turn the printed side inwards (so observers don't know what came in the box) and then take it to the recycling centre. That way nobody but you and the friends you show your new 'toy' to will know what you have.

Information theft

You should seriously consider the documents and other information that you discard, and how you dispose of documents that may be useful to a criminal. Most people have been in situations where they are asked to produce proof of identity, where household bills or perhaps bank statements are accepted. A sift through the rubbish bin of many houses will produce an alarming amount of information, such as:

- bank statements
- pay statements/slips
- CVs and job applications with full personal details on applicants
- income tax documents
- receipts for purchases containing your bank information
- cash withdrawal receipts
- insurance documents
- personal letters
- full name and date of birth
- personal loan information
- court papers
- mortgage statements and details
- utility bills
- credit card statements and receipts showing numbers and expiry dates
- council tax statements
- notes showing cash card and other card personal PIN numbers
- discarded and out-of-date credit cards.

Are you happy that strangers could have collected that sort of personal information about you and your family so easily? Are you happy that businesses are so careless with your details that they throw similar information into a bin to which anyone has access?

Do you care that strangers know what you get paid, what your regular monthly payments are, or what your bank balance is?

Other than an intrusion into your private affairs, criminals could use all of this information to run up huge bills using your name! Credit card numbers are quite handy. Some unscrupulous employees working for companies which carelessly overlook criminal transactions can earn thousands from your credit card. You may discard enough information to give them on-line access to your bank account, or deal in stolen cars!

But it gets worse! Criminals could abuse your identity in more extreme ways. With the information and papers from your dustbin they could quite easily get a duplicate of your birth certificate by pretending to be you. With that they can begin to create a parallel identity, perhaps renting accommodation and setting up bank accounts, then taking out huge mortgages or importing drugs. This process is called 'identity theft' and I saw a report that stated that during 2003, identity theft increased by 54% over the previous year. The information is all they need and it is possible that you are happily tossing that into the bin for them to take their pick.

In the UK, identity fraud in 2003 cost us a total of £1.3 billion. But it is widely reported that identity fraud is a growth criminal industry so the 2004 and subsequent figures will be a lot higher.

Criminals are happy to pay the homeless and drug addicts to search bags and bins; there has been a surge in reports of interference with rubbish bags all over the country but mainly in major cities. While searching for information they slit bags open and toss through the rubbish looking for likely information. When they get it, they can either use it or sell it on. Apparently the going rate for personal details is surprisingly low. About £5 to £30 buys you a name and address with credit card details with expiry dates, etc. A top rate of about £50 will be paid for a full range of personal information that can be used to establish an identity.

With your information being misused you could lose money from your accounts and you could find that your credit rating has fallen to a point where you can no longer get loans. People have been refused a mortgage or loan because of debts that they knew nothing about, or even had the police asking them questions about fraudulent transactions completed in their name. Don't get caught out.

Information theft – countermeasures

✔ The answer is to destroy any personal documents and you can do that in a number of ways. For example:

Scissors. You could sit and cut things up – Anything that contains personal information, such as bank account details, National Insurance numbers and your pay slips, etc. Though you could sit and snip up the whole page into tiny unreadable pieces, you only need to destroy the sections of a document that hold that personal information. You don't need to destroy the parts of a credit card statement that only tell you how to pay, or advertise and invite you to apply for a loan. If you are certain that it has no personal information on it, just throw it away!

Fire. If you have the space and time to do it safely, you could keep all of your personal documents and then have a monthly bonfire to totally destroy any trace of personal information. You have to have the space to do it safely. You have to make sure that everything has been completely destroyed and that the fire is completely out before you leave it. You also have to clean up the ashes or leave them blowing around the garden and put up with the mess!

Office shredder. Many people have access to an office shredder, and many employers do not object to their staff bringing in and shredding the occasional document, but before you try it would be best to check with your employer. If they allow you to do it, don't abuse it. Once word gets around in the family you could end up with all the personal documents for your mother, father, aunt, grandmother and your cousin Bob. Your employer would not be pleased if you were spending two hours per day destroying family documents.

Home shredder. You can buy shredders for home use. They range from hand-cranked plastic boxes to almost office specification machines starting at about £60. Most shredders are graded by how fine the strips are. The more strips you cut a page into the harder it would be to reassemble them and gather the information. A cross cut shredder is even more secure, because it not only shreds a page, it cuts each little strip into sections cutting across the strip – hence the name. That makes reassembly of a cross cut shredded page even more difficult. You can manage with a hand-cranked machine, but they are quite slow. An electric shredder is quicker and more convenient. CAUTION: remember that if abused a shredder can be dangerous and that shredded paper could be a significant fire hazard!

Security waste disposal companies. Some companies offer a secure shredding service. They have industrial shredders, and will contract to attend client premises to collect confidential documents. They contract and guarantee to collect, transport, shred and dispose of those documents in absolute security. However, most security waste disposal companies would probably not be interested in dealing with household documents and if they did the fees would be considerable.

✔ Don't give out personal information over the telephone unless you are absolutely and totally sure of the identity of the person calling. I suggest that you should never give personal details over the telephone to anyone who calls you, no matter what their reason or excuse.

✔ If you need to give personal details only do so if you telephone them, so that you are sure of their identity. If so only call them on a telephone number that you can confirm, e.g. it is on your bank statement, or is taken from a telephone directory, etc.

✔ If somebody telephones and asks for personal or financial details, NEVER call them back on the number they give you. You could be phoning a criminal. If they require details tell them to write to you, or tell them to give you a name and address so that you can look up their legitimate number in the telephone directory.

✔ Remember that the Internet is just another telephone call. Some criminals are not trying to collect personal information via emails. The email looks official and seems to come from an official source, e.g. fraudoffice@mybank.com, but they are quite easy to create. To all intents and purposes anyway, the Internet and emails are not secure, NEVER give personal, financial or any private information out over the Internet. When buying over the Internet, only do so if you are totally and absolutely sure that the website is secure and legitimate!

✔ False websites are quite easy to create as well. If I was a criminal I could create a website called www.securityyourbank.com. I could set that up to look like it was an official site run by your bank. I could entice you to log in and 'register' for reduced rates, free gifts or a chance to enter our million pound draw. Of course when you register you will have to prove you are you by keying in your account number, credit card number, security code and your mother's maiden name and the last purchase you made over £100 on that card. With all of those details, they are spending your money before you log off! NEVER give personal, financial, medical or any details over the Internet in any survey, quiz, competition or other transaction.

✔ Never trust a mail shot, it may look official but you don't know. An official looking letter arrives through your front door, explaining that everybody is switching to PIN number cards for security reasons and asking you to fill in and return the enclosed form to 'our processing centre'. So the form asks for the account number, expiry date, security code details, your mother's maiden name, etc, and you return it in the conveniently post paid envelope to Mr C Riminal, Central Processing Centre, PO Box 1554, Crookstown. There goes some more of your money!

✔ Before you fill in any form, stop and think. A lot of organisations issue forms for such things as extended warranty, or asking for a quote for a new kitchen, or whatever. Have you ever wondered why they are asking some of the questions, such as:
  ➢ Do you own your own home?
  ➢ Do you have a mortgage – if so how much?
  ➢ Which banks do you use?
  ➢ What is your annual income?

✔ They are collecting information on YOU. Nothing to do with what they are selling. They are collecting marketing information that they use or sell to other people to use. When you fill that form in, marketing men are sitting around rubbing their hands in glee. For example, they now know that you are a young married couple with no children, you own your own house and have a high income, so suddenly all sorts of marvellous offers start coming through your letterbox. Do you want to buy a luxury timeshare in Costaripoff? Do you want to buy exclusive designer handbags, or maybe a top of the range set of golf clubs?

✔ When you get a form, fill in what is pertinent and cross out the 'information gathering' questions that have no bearing on the purchase or enquiry. If they won't sell to me I will write to their head office to complain about their tactics, but I don't really care, plenty of other honest businesses will sell me their products without demanding information that they don't need!

Then they come back!

Criminals know that you will claim off your insurance and replace anything that has been stolen. They know that you will replace your missing possessions with something that is as good as, or better than what was stolen as soon as you can.

Unfortunately, having been inside they also know a bit about the security of your house, so it is quite common for criminals to wait to give you time to replace everything, then come back. On the second visit they take all the new possessions that you have only just unwrapped (another reason not to leave those boxes out for the dustman).

House Survey – Property Records

You would probably be surprised at the number of people who cannot name the make or model of valuable equipment when they are reporting a theft, let alone quote a serial number. The 'valuable contents survey' you have either just completed or will soon complete needs to be written up, stored safely and updated as your possessions change over time.

You should have a clear record listing a description, make, model, serial number, identification marks and reference to any photo or video footage you may have. For example:

Description	Make	Model	Serial Number	Unique Marks	Other Information	Photograph
Lounge televiion	Panasonic	PS/345-2v	P87-FS8650-7642-22	X shaped scratch above	38 inch flat screen	
Grandmother's clock – on dining room mantle	Wilson & Wilson	N/A	546-4	Chip on case to left of winding hole	Valued @ £2,300 Aug 1991 by Acres Antiques	Property album 3 pictures 17 through 19 plus video tape 3 at 1hr 20 mins through the tape
Digital camera Dad's room	Minolta	MD-546-3	MD-29875611	Contains chip with pictures of our dog	Taken with blue canvas camera bag	N/A

Reporting and Finding Lost Property

If you have lost something valuable you must report it to the police. I have spoken to a lot of people who have assumed that once something is stolen there is nothing else they can do, they shrug their shoulders and give up on their property assuming they will never see it again.

In their work the police recover a lot of valuable items when they make arrests and raid premises, but a large proportion cannot be traced so it has to go back to the holder (the burglar). If you haven't reported your property stolen and submitted details of make, colour, size, model, serial number and identifying marks, you can't expect to get it back again.

When you report a loss or theft, the details are entered onto databases so that the police can check the identity of property that they recover. If the details of your stolen digital camera, Rolex watch, or other valuables are on that database, they will trace them if they come to light during investigations.

This has several benefits:

- The criminal can be asked why he is in illegal possession of your valuables, a fact that can be proved by the serial number and model, etc. that you supplied.
- The criminal may well be charged with the theft or handling of your valuables.
- Best of all, once the case is closed, your property should be on its way back to you – unless the insurance has already paid out, in which case the valuables become the property of the insurance company.

If you have lost anything it is worth checking with the local police. They also record details of items that have been found so they might already be holding your valuables. Remember, without a make, model, serial number, colour, size and distinguishing marks, etc., it will be hard to claim anything!

Apart from the police databases there are a few on-line databases that you can search, for example www.trace.co.uk and www.virtualbumblebee.co.uk.

Other Issues

Everybody is unique, so there may be additional issues that are unique to you or your lifestyle and which should be included in your survey. For example, you may own a stable and horses on a field over the road, or you may own a vintage car that you keep in a commercial store. It is possible that you could run dressmaking classes from a converted barn on your property, or that you have a public right of way that runs through your garden.

Your house security audit will be compromised if you ignore any of these unique issues relating to your house and lifestyle. Take some time to make sure that you have identified everything. It is easier to do that when surveying your own house because you have an intimate knowledge of it. It becomes a lot more difficult when you are performing a survey on a house you are thinking of buying, but you have to rely on the present owner's answers. If they choose to hide the fact that a public right of way runs through the front door and out through the patio doors in the dining room, your security review is seriously compromised.

The fundamental concept is to be as thorough and conscientious as possible when completing your house security review, and keep an open mind as to other issues that you should address.

Medical problems

It is possible that you may have medical conditions that affect your life, mobility or even your use of the house. For example, an elderly disabled widow may stop using the upper floors of her house if the stairs begin to cause her a problem. An elderly man on limited income may retreat to live in the kitchen in a very cold winter because that is the easiest room to keep warm. A disabled couple may never go into their garage, and a deaf person wouldn't hear any breaking glass or disturbance in the next room.

The reason changes from person to person, but the effect on the way people live and use their homes can be significant. Due to circumstances and frailty, some elderly people might not know that they had been burgled for weeks, for example if they never go upstairs, or never go into the front room in winter. Be sure to tailor your review to the way you live your life, and if doing a review for an elderly relative take all of their circumstances into consideration.

Building work

Remember that if you employ builders or decorators to work on your home, you will have a range of new security problems. For example:

- You will have to give reasonable access to the builders or decorators.
- They may well store valuable materials or tools around the property, which could attract criminal interest.
- If they erect any scaffold or ladders, they will significantly reduce the security of your house.

83

Building work – countermeasures

✔ If you are going to employ any builders or decorators, insist that they should provide you with:
  ➤ references as to the quality of their work
  ➤ references as to their ability to finish work within stated time, cost and quality targets
  ➤ assurances as to the honesty and integrity of their employees
  ➤ proof of insurance, which covers you, your family and property for any injury, loss, damage caused by his or his employees' and agents' oversight, actions, negligence, accident or criminal acts.

✔ Before you accept any bids and quotes, check all references supplied.

✔ Before the builders arrive make every effort to remove valuables from any areas they will have access to.

✔ Never leave builders or other workers alone in the home, and certainly do not give them any keys to the premises.

✔ When you arrange for the work to be done, arrange matters so that you or an adult member of the family are always at home watching to check on security, safety and the type and quality of the work being done.

✔ By all means pay a deposit, but never pay for a job until it has been finished *to your satisfaction*.

✔ As a general rule never employ workmen who knock on your door! If they don't have a genuine address that you can check, established offices or yard, don't use them!

House insurance

If you have decided to take the time to make your house as safe as you can, I suspect you are the sort of person who would think that investing in insurance cover would be worthwhile.

The insurance industry operates on 'chances' and 'odds'. If you want to insure yourself against a specific occurrence, an insurance company will look at the risk, calculate the chances of that happening, calculate what they would have to pay out if they had to pay on a claim and set a fee from there.

Broadly speaking there are two different types of household cover.

Building insurance
You can insure the structure of the building. This means if the house burns to the ground, the insurance company will pay for it to be rebuilt in the same style. Warning: you should check the coverage supplied by your insurer. In some circumstances an insurer might specify conditions under which they will not cover your property against damage.

The basis of payments following an insured loss vary. Generally with buildings insurance, the structure will be replaced, to the same design and style as the original house, though it will comply with modern building regulations. Don't expect two extra bedrooms and a swimming pool, you will get a new house of the same size and plan as the original.

Potential problems include:

- **Flood** – with weather patterns changing and sea levels rising there is an increasing risk of flooding. In some areas on historical flood plains, properties have been built on areas that have often been subject to flooding. When these areas are built up and paved, there is even less chance for water to flow off naturally so flooding is ever more likely. In these circumstances an insurer might refuse to cover a specific property or area for flood damage.
- **Subsidence** – some areas are prone to subsidence. Properties built over old mine workings, or in areas where there are underlying clay beds, often subside, causing damage to houses. If an insurer knows that a high proportion if not all properties in a given area will suffer damage from subsidence, they will refuse to insure them against damage caused by subsidence, or charge huge premiums.
- **Fire** – though they are usually seen abroad, forest and bush fires can be a problem. In areas where bush fires are common insurers can refuse to insure a property against fire damage. With climate changes this could eventually become a problem in some areas of the UK.

Building insurance – countermeasures

✔ Before buying a property you should check with the current owner, the estate agent, the local authority and a few insurance companies to find out if there are any insurance restrictions on the property in question.

✔ Flooding problems:
  ➢ Don't buy a house that is at risk of flooding!
  ➢ Check the environment agency floodplain maps on www.environment-agency.gov.uk.
  ➢ If you are in an area where flooding is possible, minimise your risks. Don't install expensive equipment on the ground floor. Don't leave your property unattended when there is risk of flooding. Always call the flood lines to check what the local flooding risk is, and take preventative and precautionary measures when needed. See www.environment-agency.gov.uk.
  ➢ If a flood is possible, move vulnerable people, pets and valuables to safety. Move cars to safety on higher ground. Unplug electrical equipment and take it upstairs (television, video recorder, sound system, fridge freezer, washing machine, etc.).

➤ If your neighbours don't seem to be doing anything, especially if they are elderly or infirm, take the time to make sure that they know there is a flood alert.

➤ Make sure that your insurance certificate and contact numbers are available and safe (on the top floor) so that you can easily make contact to clear up afterwards.

➤ Be ready to wait out the flood, you will need to move food and bottled water (mains supplies may be contaminated with sewage) to an upper floor. Remember there will probably be no power available, so stock up with tinned and dried food and a gas heater.

➤ Beware of the use of candles and camping stoves – the last thing you want in a flood is a fire because the fire and rescue services won't be able to reach you. Have fire extinguishers handy.

➤ Make sure you have adequate supplies of baby food (if you have not been able to take a baby or small children to safety at a relative's or friend's house).

➤ Make sure that you have enough medication and a first aid kit ready for use. You don't want to be cut off and then discover that you urgently need more insulin or other medication.

➤ To prevent back flow from a flood, stuff a sandbag down downstairs toilets. (Back flow is where flooding pushes waste up out of sewers and drains into toilets, baths and sinks.) Put a bung or plug in any sinks or baths and weight them down with a sandbag or two to prevent back flow.

➤ If possible turn the electricity and gas off at the mains – and don't turn it on again until the flood has subsided and it has been checked and approved by a qualified inspector.

✔ If there is a restriction put on the insurance cover of a property, you should make every effort to find out why and very seriously consider if you want to take the risk of buying an 'uninsurable' property.

✔ If you already own a property with insurance restrictions, find out exactly what those restrictions are and why they were imposed on the property. Discover what the risks are and then make every effort to ensure that you reduce the risks to the property where you can. For example, if there is a fire hazard, cut back shrubbery, lay gravel around the property and possibly connect up external high-pressure sprinklers that will spray the house and surrounding area if there is a fire. If subsidence is a problem, beware of operations that extract water from the surrounding land. For example, don't use a bore hole pump to extract water to water the garden and as some plants and trees are known to be very thirsty, take expert advice on what you plant close to and around the property.

✔ If a neighbour starts to redesign their garden, radically changing levels and drainage that affect you, you should discuss the problem with them. Similarly, if they start planting a willow or other very thirsty tree you should point out the possible problems and come to some arrangement. In extreme cases, you may have to go to court to prevent the work being done, to protect your property.

Contents insurance

You can also insure the contents of the house. That is the carpets, curtains, beds, clothes, television, washing machine, camera, CD collection – anything contained in the house, the contents! If the house burns down, a 'contents' policy will pay for replacements for everything that was lost.

Note: The chances of an accident happening vary, depending on a huge number of variables. The easiest example is to look at a thatched cottage and a cottage with a slate roof. If there is a fire the thatched cottage will burn quickly and the cost of repair will be high. The cottage with the slate roof is less likely to burn and will not suffer such extreme damage from a roof fire because it will spread slower in a slate roof. In that case it's fair that anyone with a thatched roof will pay higher insurance fees than if they had a slate roof.

But there are a lot of different variables that affect the risk of an accident happening and all of these are taken into account when calculating odds and cost, which are considered by the insurer to set their fees.

The basis of payments on contents insurance varies so much that you must carefully review what insurance you require then compare that with what you actually have. One problem is that insurance policies are written in such a complex way that they are beyond the understanding of an average person. You might think you know what it seems to mean in plain English, but in legal terms it may mean something different. I suggest that you should discuss the matter with your insurance broker, and get them to explain and answer your questions.

Potential insurance problems include:

- **Inadequate cover.** Most people steadily acquire new possessions and over time upgrade existing possessions. As new inventions come onto the market, many of us will buy them. Ten years ago, most families might not have had a CD player at home, they certainly wouldn't have had a DVD player or an ipod. If you haven't reviewed the level of your insurance cover for a while you should check to make sure that you are adequately covered.
- **Not new for old.** Some insurance policies specify that contents will be replaced on a new for old basis. That means that a 26 inch Sanyo colour television will be replaced by a new 26 inch Sanyo colour television. Without new for old, you will only receive what the insurance company decides was the value of the set at the time of the loss. For example, say you paid £500 when your television was new, but it is now three years old. Your insurance company might state that the value of that set on the day it was lost or destroyed was only £95, and that is all they will pay. You have no television, a new set will now cost

£600, but all you receive from the insurance company is £95, so you cannot afford to replace the television even with the insurance pay out!

- **Single item limit.** It is possible that your insurance cover specifies a limit to the value of single items covered under the general policy. For example, an insurance company might state that all general items are limited to a maximum individual value of £750. That doesn't sound as though it is a problem until you start looking at the items that cost more than that. Home computers, washer dryers and wide screen televisions are a few of the items that can easily cost more than £1,000. If your policy does state a limit, you will lose out if you have to make a claim.

- **Valuable items not listed.** Where an insurance policy has a general limit set on the value of single items, the insurance company might for an additional fee offer extra cover on named items. For example, you can insure the general contents of your home and accept the single item limit of £750, and then add the more expensive items such as your £3,000 flat screen plasma television as separate listed items. If you forget to mention to the insurance company that you have a work of art worth £2.5 million you will have to make special arrangements with the insurance company and meet their stated minimum security requirements.

- **Exemptions.** Some policies impose exemptions. For example, your flat screen plasma television will be insured only when it is in your home. If you take the television to work so that your colleagues can watch a cup final football match in their lunch break, the television might not be insured from the time you take it out through your front door until you bring it back. Bicycles, cameras, watches and jewellery may not be covered outside of the premises.

- **Negligence.** It is possible that the insurer has the right to refuse to meet a claim where they can claim that you were negligent. For example, if you go to work and leave the lights on and the front door open, you may not be able to claim if you come home nine hours later and find that your property has been stolen.

Contents insurance – countermeasures

✔ Check the value of the contents of your home and make sure that your level of insurance cover is adequate to replace everything. Though it may sound difficult, it is quite easy to check the value of the contents of your home. Take a notebook, and move from room to room making a note of the value of items in some basic categories, making sure that you do not include items in more than one category. For example, the categories could be:

Furnishings – chair, cushion, cupboard, table, sofa, curtains, carpets, rugs, etc.

Electrical – washing machine, TV, DVD, computer, vacuum cleaner, microwave oven, etc.

Clothing – outerwear, underwear, hats, boots and shoes, formal wear, leisure wear, etc.

Possessions – watches, makeup, books, briefcase, handbag, etc.

Valuables – jewellery, stamp collection, antique clock, medals, etc.

✔ When you have made a thorough list of the items present in each room, not forgetting to look in cupboards and drawers, as well as the loft and the cellar, you should leave it for a day or so. You won't be adding every single shirt or pair of high heels to the list, just add a category such as shirts x 20, or heels x 12. Then a day or so later go back and walking around the house review the list with a fresh eye. Add anything that comes to light – for example – when you checked your wife may have been using the digital camera, and that reminds you of your video camera that you loaned to Mrs Biggins for her daughter's wedding. When that is finally completed you have to assign a **replacement value** to everything on the list. The replacement value is how much it will cost to buy a similar item today! You will then have a replacement value and contents list of everything in each room (which you could cross check against your serial number list to make sure you have everything). From there it is easy to add up a total replacement value for all your possessions in the house!

✔ Having arrived at a replacement cost at 'current' prices, you can check that your insurance policy offers 'new for old' replacement. If they don't, start negotiating. Just as a ten-minute exercise to reinforce the importance of new for old, do a few calculations on a copy of your pricing list. For example, those 20 shirts may have cost you £30 each, so replacement as new cost is £600. But if the insurance values them at current value, shirts in Oxfam are 50 pence so the insurance company would pay 20 x 50 pence which comes to £10, which is not enough to buy one new shirt. Those high heels all cost £300 per pair, but the second-hand value taken from a local newspaper is £25 per pair. That means we lost 12 pairs at £300 per pair, a total cost of £3,600, but the insurance will only pay out 12 x £25 = £300 – enough to buy one pair of shoes!

✔ Check your pricing list against any single item price limit. If there is a problem, talk to the insurance company and resolve the problem as soon as you can (and always get any changes in writing).

✔ If you have any particularly valuable items, make sure that your insurance policy actually covers them.

✔ Check your policy and be aware of any exemptions to the insurance cover. If limits or restrictions are placed on you, keep them in mind to retain adequate cover.

✔ Insurance companies may refuse to pay out on claims where the insured person has been negligent in caring for or protecting their property. By reading this book, learning the lessons and following the advice set out in it, your security awareness and controls should ensure that you never suffer loss due to your negligence.

House manual

Not many houses have one, but if one exists take a look at it. If you are surveying your house and you don't have a house manual, consider producing one!

A house manual contains important information about and relating to the house. I propose that a house manual should be produced using a four-ring binder. In that way sections that change can easily be replaced, and if a section is needed in an emergency, it can be taken out and used, then put back into the house manual.

Emergency pages should be laminated; that will keep them readable even if you do need to take the manual into the kitchen when the washing machine is flooding the ground floor.

I suggest that the house manual should contain the following sections, and any other information appropriate to you and your lifestyle.

Emergency information

This section should be in alphabetic order. One entry to a page and all entries in large print that will be easy to see when your eyes are blurry at three in the morning, your loft tank starts to leak and you have to read by moonlight because the lights have fused!

All pages should be updated when there are changes. Where explanations are difficult, you could include annotated photographs affixed to the laminated page, to illustrate a point – for example, which of five stopcocks at the back of the linen closet turns off the water supply to the central heating? As well as information such as:

• Water stop cocks – water supply, central heating, washing machine, etc.
• Mains power switch and other power isolation switches and fuses
• Emergency glazing service
• Veterinary surgery – assuming you have pets

Contact information

This section should contain contact information. It should be in alphabetic order and could be multiple entry. (By multiple entry, I mean that you put in 'sensible' entries. For example, you might put in an entry under S for Splatter & Son who are your decorators. In case you forget their name you could also put an entry under D reading *Decorators – Splatter & Son*, so you will be able to find the number if you look up 'Splatter & Son' or look up 'Decorator').

Any information you might require should be contained within the manual:

decorators, builders, garden services, car maintenance, electricians, etc. The 'contacts' section of the house manual then becomes valuable to you.

Significant dates

This section is more like a diary for the house. In it you will record any significant events relating to the house. For example:

Date	Event	Contact	Comment
2/7/1998	Whole house rewired	Live 'N Kicking electricians contact Bob Jones	1 Year guarantee expires 1/7/1999
11/4/2000	Double glazing installed	Take A Butchers – double glazing company	5 year guarantee expires 10/4/2005

This information will be helpful to you if you need to remember when things were completed. If you have a problem you will quickly be able to check back to see if the gas fire is still under guarantee and who you need to contact.

Unique selling point

The house manual will be a unique selling point for your house should you ever decide to sell it. It will contain a lot of information that will be invaluable to the new owner.

Imagine how impressed you would be if a house owner presented you with a nice tidy house manual. It shows that you are organised and efficient. It shows that you have taken care of the house and the records relating to it, so you have almost certainly been as efficient in ensuring that all work undertaken has been of an acceptable quality and standard.

More than that, the manual contains the details of honest and trustworthy tradespeople in the area, which is a very rare and valuable commodity to most people.

Better than that, it lists who you use and therefore obviously consider to be the best and best value for money: veterinary surgery, pet store, butcher, fishmonger, garden centre, supermarket and any other local services.

3 Security When Away

■ ■

Most people go away for a few weeks' holiday each year. When you are away and your house is unattended it is vulnerable. There are some basic precautions which you should take.

Remember Security
■ ■

In the excitement of planning your holiday remember that you should be making your holiday arrangements with the security of your house in mind.

Think ahead – deliveries

When approaching holiday times, in everything you do remember that you are planning to be away between given dates. Avoid ordering anything that may be delivered when you are away. When you do place orders, make sure that even if the delivery is later than the suppliers have promised, any goods you order will all be delivered before you go away.

If you have any doubts that a delivery will be made before you leave, or want to order something that will arrive while you are away, ask a neighbour or family member if you can have it delivered to their house.

Don't under any circumstances have it delivered to your home address. Packages waiting on doorsteps are tempting to a casual thief, as well as advertising to a whole range of people that you are not at home and may not be around for a few days.

Deliveries – countermeasures

✔ Avoid ordering anything that will be delivered while you are away.

✔ If you have to order something for delivery while you are away, ask for it to be delivered to a relative or trustworthy neighbour.

✔ Try to arrange for a relation or trusted neighbour to come to the house each day to check for mail or other items delivered and left on the doorstep or filling the letterbox.

Leaving notes

No matter what the excuse, never, ever leave a note on the door. Notes such as 'Milkman – we are on holiday – no milk until 18th August', or perhaps 'On holiday until 18th August ALL Deliveries to Number 7 Please' are a gift to criminals. Remember even a note saying 'gone to shops back in five minutes' may be enough to tempt a burglar.

Leaving notes – countermeasures

✔ Arrange matters so that a note will not be necessary, by making sure that deliveries are all made before you go and regular deliveries are cancelled.

✔ If you know and trust the milkman tell him that you don't want any milk until the 18th of August, but don't ever leave a note advertising that fact to everyone.

✔ If you don't know or trust the milkman, consider NOT cancelling the milk! It will cost you a few pounds but as long as you can arrange for a relative or trusted neighbour to collect your daily milk delivery and use it while you are away, the milkman will be none the wiser.

✔ If possible arrange for a trusted relative to collect the mail. Consider removing any mail basket inside the letterbox for the duration of your absence, particularly if you receive a lot of mail!

Junk mail and circulars

Your letterbox and front step are important to maintaining your security. For a few weeks before your departure keep an eye on what is delivered. Not just the usual post and milk, it is the 'unwanted deliveries' that could be a problem. Free newspapers, circulars, flyers and pizza advertisements all flow through my letter-box or more often are just dumped onto the doorstep. I haven't asked for any of them, I have no interest in them and they all go straight into the rubbish bin. Unfortunately, these are the deliveries that can cause you problems.

If not collected and disposed of, within a few days they could overflow your letterbox and doorstep, cascading out to blow around the garden for all to see. This is a clear indication that you are not at home and, by the time the doorstep is stacked up with this rubbish you clearly haven't been there for some days. That will attract the attention of the local criminals.

In my area a free newspaper is published and supposed to be delivered every Wednesday, but it is actually usually delivered on a Saturday or Sunday by youngsters who cannot be bothered to push it though a letterbox. They fling it onto the doorstep in any weather, where it either gets soaked or blows around the garden. Worse than that it frequently contains other mail shots, which the ill-advised advertisers have paid to be delivered on the issue date.

I contacted the circulation manager of the publisher to complain, but she wasn't interested. I tried to contact somebody with more seniority in her organisation, but I was brushed off, so I contacted some of the advertisers. I collected a handful of the delayed mail shots in the next issue and looked through them. Some were advertising special promotions and offers that had finished by the time the paper was delivered so I began calling those companies. I asked about the offers to check that they had expired, then asked if they knew that their advertising material had been circulated late, after their closing date. I asked if they were happy that their advertising handouts were dumped on doorsteps and not pushed through letterboxes. I asked if they cared that because of the late delivery and careless handling households by their association with the publishers of the free paper people were feeling annoyed with them and their products. I gave my name and told them I would be willing to support any claim they may want to make against the distributors.

Within a week I had a phone call from a smarmy man who introduced himself as a senior executive with the publishers of the free paper. He assured me that the past problems had been resolved and that a number of delivery staff had been disciplined. For a couple of weeks things were fine then they went back to their old ways, this time the free paper took my call, and this time they removed me from their circulation list, so I am not bothered with their annoying and forest denuding trash any more!

Whatever you do, make sure that while you have carefully managed and cancelled all deliveries this junk mail doesn't spoil all your good work. Where possible get somebody to check the property each day, and if possible spend a few hours there, to make the place look lived in. Remember to make absolutely sure that they secure the house when they leave though!

Junk mail and circulars – countermeasures

✔ Try to make sure that your mail is cleared each day while you are away. If a few bulky circulars are forced through your letterbox, they can block future deliveries. The postman may take new deliveries back to the sorting office to await collection when you return, but people delivering free newspapers and junk mail circulars will almost certainly simply dump new deliveries at and around the front door and doorstep.

✔ I did see a house that had a special delivery slot for circulars and free newspapers. Actually it was a large box with a lid and a wide access slot, sited near the front door. The owner told me that inside the box was a plastic crate. A couple of times a week he would take the crate out of the 'circulars mail box' remove each item and throw it into his recycling bin. He only checked it in case some genuine post had been put there in error.

✔ If you would like to try to stop junk mail being sent to you by direct marketing organisations, you could try contacting the Mail Preference Service. Please see www.mpsonline.org.uk for details and to register your desire to be excluded from junk mail postings. It doesn't stop all junk mail but it considerably reduces it. You will need a valid email address to complete the on-line process and they warn that it can take up to four months to have full effect. (www.fpsonline.org.uk for details and to register your desire to be excluded from junk fax advertising, www.tpsonline.org.uk for details and to register your desire to be excluded from unsolicited telephone advertising).

✔ A similar organisation which deals with telephone marketing is the Telephone Preference Service, which can be contacted on 0845 0700707 or by emailing tps@dma.org.uk. All you have to do is register your phone numbers and you should be excluded from most UK telephone marketing.

Central heating

If you are going on a winter holiday you may have to leave your heating on so that the water pipes are protected from frost damage. A low setting will not use too much fuel, but it will prevent the pipes from freezing and keep the house safe and comfortable for your return.

Central heating – countermeasures

✔ Make sure that your central heating system has been properly serviced and maintained. If it is, you can be pretty sure that it will not cause a fire or leak and flood your house while you are away.

✔ If going away in winter you should consider leaving your central heating on at a low level to prevent the pipes from freezing. This will also keep the house dry and fairly warm for your return.

Lights on timers

Whenever you are away, you should try to make the house look as occupied and lived in as possible. Any action you can take to make it appear as though somebody is around will be an extra deterrent to a criminal who is considering targeting your house.

A number of manufacturers supply electrical timers. They plug into an electrical socket and you can plug a light or other device into them. The timers then work off the electricity, and at set times programmed by you, they will switch the device plugged into them on and off. So you can make a light come on and go off at times you have set.

The better electrical timers have a battery backup function. Without the battery, in a power cut the timer could lose its programmed operation and stop working, or carry on working with a clock that was running a few hours late. That could make lights come off and on in the early hours of the morning, which would attract the attention of criminals rather than put them off.

Lights on timers – countermeasures

✔ Make sure that you only buy safe and approved electrical timers, something that will not cause a fire while they are unattended.

✔ Use them sparingly. Don't make your house look like seaside illuminations with all sorts of things switching on and off at different times.

✔ Make sure that you have some lights that can be operated by the timers, such as standard and table lamps.

✔ The timer light will look better if you can get a relative to go to your house and draw the curtains in the evening and open them again in the morning when they come to collect the milk and gather up the post, etc.

✔ Use them strategically, and make sure that you plan their use. I suggest that their use should follow your lifestyle pattern. For example, if you wake up at six each morning, have a bedroom light that comes on at six. If you sit in the lounge from five until ten then go to bed, I would suggest that the timers are used to switch the lounge lights on at five and switch them off at ten, while the bedroom timer light comes on at ten to ten and goes off at quarter past ten. This should give the indication of the normal pattern of use, so to a casual observer there is no clue that you are away. Depending on your window dressing you may have to ask the relative or neighbour who is checking for junk mail to make their visit in the early evening when they can close the curtains, then come back in the morning to open them again.

Radio talk stations

Just as the lights above give the illusion of occupancy, leaving a radio on could help your illusion, depending on how you use it. I put a radio onto one of the timer switches, and arrange for the radio to be tuned to a talk station. Music stations are OK, but an intruder won't be fooled into thinking that 20 current pop stars are staying at your house if he hears their music. On the other hand, if you tune the radio to a talk station, all he will be able to hear from the outside is muffled voices, from which he cannot be sure if there are actually people in the house talking.

That uncertainty should be enough to make him look for an easier and safer target down the road.

Radio talk station – countermeasures

✔ Buy or keep a timer switch to operate the radio.

✔ Tune the radio to a station that you know will be all talk.

✔ News and current affairs discussion channels are acceptable, because the participants are usually fairly unknown. A channel with a well-known and recognisable celebrity talking won't fool the criminals.

✔ Tune the radio accurately, as a crackling badly tuned hissing station will not fool anyone.

✔ Set the volume to a subdued conversational level, don't be tempted to turn it up so that the criminals 'will definitely be able to hear it'. If it is too loud they will know what it is.

The garden

Don't forget that your garden can tell tales on you too. An uncut and overgrown lawn is very obvious to anyone passing by. If the hanging baskets are wilting through lack of water, or weeds have invaded the flowerbeds, you are giving the criminals more indications that nobody is home. If you usually trim the hedge every Sunday then suddenly it is left to grow for two weeks in August it will be noticed and the criminals will draw their own conclusions from the change!

Garden based evidence alone can point to a family on holiday. Add the extra information about the lack of activity in the house, the milkman doesn't stop there any more, there aren't any kids playing in the garden, and you begin to see that it is quite difficult to hide your absence from anyone who regularly passes by. It might take them ten days to notice, but eventually the evidence builds up to the inescapable conclusion that you are away and the house is empty.

Garden – countermeasures

✔ Arrange for a neighbour to water the hanging baskets, tubs and borders so that the plants don't wilt and die, drawing attention to the empty house.

✔ Make sure that you give the lawn and hedge an extra trim the day before you go on holiday. Pull out the weeds and water the garden thoroughly. That will delay the onset of an unkempt appearance.

✔ Possibly arrange for a friend to enter the house and make it look lived in for a few hours every now and then. I know of one lady who asks her neighbour to go into her house a couple of times a week to tend to the house plants, then to watch television for a few hours, so that people can see life and activity in the house.

✔ If you have children, you may ask your friend or neighbour to move things around when they are there. That can be done while watering the garden or mowing the grass to make it look innocent but the idea is to move children's bikes and toys, etc. If the kids' bikes and toys stay in one place for a week or two it will be noticed, move things around and the house and garden look normal and in use.

✔ Make sure sheds are locked, cars are in garages with secondary security devices fitted and that the garages themselves are secured.

✔ Make sure that all ladders, tools and any equipment that could be stolen or used to break into your home, are securely locked away.

Refuse collection

When making your arrangements don't forget the dustman. Here is another task for that visiting relative or friendly neighbour. In the first week you will have rubbish in your bin that you don't want to leave to decompose and rot for the time you are away. Neither do you want a passing criminal to notice and investigate why all the houses in the street have put their dustbin out – except you!

You should arrange for somebody to put the dustbin out and take it in when it has been emptied. In the first week all will then appear to be normal to the passing burglar. In the second and any subsequent weeks, ask the visitor to bring a few bags of rubbish, put them in your bin and put it out for collection as normal. This should maintain another little bit of the illusion that somebody is still at home and that the house is not empty and vulnerable.

Remember these things may be minor, but every single action helps to build on and reinforce the illusion that you are still at home!

Refuse collection – countermeasures

✔ If at all possible make things appear as normal as they can be to passing criminals, including putting the bin out and taking it in as usual.

✔ You should have arranged for somebody to visit your house every day to take junk mail off the step, look after the garden and generally make the house appear to be in use. They should also put the dustbin out the first week. In subsequent weeks they should put junk mail and rubbish into the bin and put it out for the dustman.

✔ Ideally the person visiting the house must have time to spend an hour or so at the house, following the normal pattern of the homeowner. The dustbin should be put out and taken in following the same pattern as normal. If it is usually put out the night before, then do the same while the homeowner is away. If the bin is usually emptied and taken in about mid afternoon, then as far as is possible that should be kept up. You are trying to maintain a normal appearance! If a harassed relative races up in his car and screeches to a halt minutes before the dustman arrives and then races off back to work in a cloud of tyre smoke it will have totally the opposite effect to the one you are planning. That sort of behaviour will draw attention to your house. Just like milk piled up on a doorstep, or mail overflowing from a letterbox, a dustbin left out overnight is a clear sign that nobody is home. A burglar will soon notice that and take action to investigate further.

Don't give information away

You have hopefully made your house and property as secure as you can and your car is locked away and secure in the garage. Now that you are going away, will you tell all of the local criminals that you won't be at home for two weeks because you will be on the beach in Barbados or driving across America?

Well you say you won't, but are you *sure* you won't be telling them that? You are excited about your holiday and are happy to tell family and friends, neighbours and colleagues at work, all about your imminent adventure. Can you trust all of them? Even if you can trust all of them, who might they mention your holiday plans to? How many people know about your holiday plans? Take a moment to consider the question and mentally add any names to the list below.

• You told the milkman because you had to cancel the milk and because he was impressed with your proposed trip to Barbados, he has told everyone at the depot – then they told their friends and family so you have to consider them as well.

- You told the newsagent and his staff, then there are the 15 paperboys and their families. When you were telling the newsagent, there were three other people in the shop at the time and they all told their friends and family.
- The travel agent and staff know, of course, plus anyone they told and anyone else who was in the shop at the time!
- The bank employees where you got your foreign currency and travellers cheques all know.
- The doctor and their staff know, because you had to enquire about vaccinations and first aid, then book and have your vaccinations.
- Everyone where you work knows, plus at least a few customers and suppliers!
- Everyone at the local pub and anyone they speak to now know.
- Not forgetting everyone at the local taxi company and they even know the date, time and flight numbers of your departure and return!

So, without too much trouble we have identified a minimum of one hundred people who know that you will be out of the country for two weeks starting on the 14th. Are you happy with that?

If you do speak to your neighbour you don't know who is listening. Take a moment to consider how easy it could be. Perhaps unfortunately and unknown to you, when you were talking to Mrs Biggins a prolific burglar was sitting in the seat behind you on the bus. He heard what you said about your holiday so he got off the bus and followed you home. Now he knows where you live and he knows that you will be away for two weeks starting on the 14th. He knows that you will be in Barbados and that you live in the really nice house he followed you to, so he thinks it will definitely be well worth him coming back in the early hours of the 16th. Is that good?

When the taxi comes to collect you and take you to the airport, you quite happily say to this strange man, take us to terminal four and then collect us again from the Barbados flight that lands at Heathrow at 19:35 on the 29th. Are you happy that you just told a stranger that your house is empty until then?

It is incredibly easy for information about your holiday absence to get into the wrong hands, but what can you do about it?

Information – countermeasures

✔ Limit the number of people who know about your holiday. There will be plenty of boasting time when you come back with loads of holiday snaps and that tasteful straw donkey!

✔ If possible get a relative to take you to the airport and collect you again on your return, then you won't have to tell any taxi drivers.

✔ If you have to take a taxi, don't tell the taxi company or driver how long you will be gone and consider using a different company to collect you from the airport on your return (that way nobody knows how long you will be gone). You could consider asking a relative to book the return taxi a day or so before your return, so even if they have criminal contacts they have little warning about your empty property and little opportunity to do anything about it.

✔ It may be considered rude but I tend not to talk to a taxi driver about anything other than the weather and traffic. He may be simply talkative, he may just be nosy, but he may be pumping me for details that I don't really want him to have.

✔ If you have to use the same company for the journey to the airport and home again consider doing some acting! Without going over the top in your acting debut, make them think somebody is still at home when you leave. For example, wait until the driver is moving and therefore can't pay too much attention to the house and then wave at your house and say something to your partner like 'Look there's Colin, he said he wouldn't wave us off.' Or perhaps 'Gosh, I didn't think Frank was ever going to let us go.' Hopefully you will have said and done enough to make the taxi driver think that there is somebody still living in the house. That means that even if he was thinking of coming back to liberate a few of your most valuable possessions late that night, he should think again.

✔ Don't put your home address on your outbound luggage tickets. They are an advert to anyone at the airport that you are going abroad and any burglars could treat the departure lounge as a pick and mix burglary counter. Once again the criminal can read you! Expensive luggage, booked on the scheduled flight to Barbados, home in the posh district of Commuterville – it won't take him long to spot the worthwhile targets. Have two luggage tickets, the outward bound ticket showing the holiday hotel address, then the return ticket that you put on before coming to the airport to come home again, which can show your home address. (I doubt if burglars have gone international yet, so anyone in the terminal in Barbados or wherever you are going won't be on the phone to his cousin Jimmy telling him to nip round to burgle your house.)

House sitter

Pets have to be considered when taking a holiday, and while some people are happy to bear the cost of putting their dog or cat in a boarding kennel, others arrange for a house sitter to take care of the house and their pets. This has the double benefit of keeping the house lived in and secure, as well as keeping the pets at home in familiar surroundings.

Boarding and kennel rates of £9 to £12 per day for a large dog and £6 per day for a cat are not uncommon and certainly not the most expensive I have seen quoted. Individually they don't seem too high, but when some kennels charge extra for insurance, heated accommodation and special diets the price soon adds up. The cost of boarding a family dog or cat while you are away on a two-week holiday could quite easily reach £250.

When the cost can be as high or higher than that, inviting somebody to stay at your house begins to make sense, especially if you have a couple of dogs and a cat! You will, however, have to ensure that they are trustworthy and will maintain your security standards while you are away. It is pointless making your house secure if for two weeks of the year your nephew Trevor Biggins leaves doors and windows open, holds open house parties and can't quite get the hang of not leaving the keys in your car!

House sitter – countermeasures

✔ If you are wealthy and have a lot of valuable possessions, your house will be a lot more secure when you are away on holiday or business trips if somebody is living in your house.

✔ It is possible to hire somebody as a house sitter, but you will have to be very sure of their credentials before you hand over the keys. I suggest that you only let a relative stay in the house and look after it. A relative is a known quantity so should be easier to select, easier to arrange and more trustworthy than a stranger.

✔ If you have any pets, bringing in a house/pet sitter could make sound financial sense. Apart from saving hundreds of pounds in pet boarding fees, you get the extra security of somebody living in the house. (An additional benefit is that the pets are happier because they get to stay at home.)

✔ If you do organise a house/pet sitter, you must be very certain that the sitter is honest and trustworthy, and that they are as careful with home security as you would be.

Create an illusion of activity

There are some things that can be done to add to the illusion of life and activity at your empty home. I have given a couple of examples. Knowing your own home, family and personal circumstances see if you can add a few illusions of your own.

Illusion of activity – countermeasures

✔ Depending on your relationship with your neighbour, you could invite them to occasionally park a car in your drive or outside your house to increase the illusion that there is activity in, around and associated with your empty house.

✔ If safe and appropriate, you could ask a neighbour to allow their children to play in your garden occasionally. You might wish to ask a visiting gardener, or the relative who is collecting your milk and checking for unwanted mail and circulars, to bring their children with them to boost the illusion of occupancy.

✔ Remember that carefully rationed acting will help as well! When the man who looks after your garden is leaving, he could stand at the gate and pretend to be holding a *short* conversation with you! For example he could pretend to be answering a question and call something like 'OK, I'll check to see if I can get a couple of those roses, see you next week' towards the back of the house. If the acting is low key and only tried once a week it should help. If the acting is bad and overdone it will draw attention to the empty house.

Careful departure

Think security in everything you do. Don't make a grandstand play out of leaving for the airport! It is pointless taking all of these security steps to make people think you are still at home, if you make so much noise and fuss about leaving that half the county can't help knowing that you have gone to the airport with three large suitcases.

If Uncle George is taking you to the airport get him to reverse up to the house and slip the cases into the boot with as few people seeing them as you can. If you are going in a taxi, try to arrange for a time when there won't be a big audience watching you. If everyone drives past your house on the way to work between 8 and 9 in the morning, try to arrange for the taxi to collect you before 8 or after 9, that way fewer people will see you leave with your obvious holiday cases.

General holiday security advice

For your peace of mind more than anything else, define a routine for closing the house while you are away. You already know that you have to cancel the milk, cut the grass, arrange for deliveries to be made before you go, etc., but look beyond that.

You don't want to get to the airport or be sitting in some Aztec ruin in the Andes worrying about household security. Think of the stress you would suffer if you couldn't quite remember if you had turned off the kitchen tap when you had a glass of water before you left, or if anyone ever actually shut the back door when Uncle George arrived to take you to the airport.

Define a procedure, list or method that will take you from room to room, to secure the house, switch on the electric timers that will operate lights and the radio, close the bedroom windows, lock the side gate, etc.

If you do that, and then follow that procedure or list in good time before your transport arrives, your should be able to avoid those nagging worries and enjoy your holiday.

✔ Pay particular attention to securing the house when you are leaving for more than a few hours, particularly when going on holiday.

✔ If a relative or neighbour will be visiting the house and will actually have access to the building, make sure that they know how to secure the house properly. I once attended a burglary where the burglar had come in through a rear door that was not locked. The owners were on holiday, the neighbour was clearing post and checking the house but couldn't get the back door to lock so she left it unlocked. The owners had forgotten to say that the lock on the back door was damaged, and you had to push the key in, half turn it then pull on the key and fully turn it to lock the door. Their failure to replace the lock before they went and their oversight in not explaining about the lock lost them some valuables and the insurance refused to pay out because the house wasn't secure.

Long holidays and business trips

There are ways of covering up a holiday that lasts a couple of weeks, but longer holidays and long business trips present some unique problems and are harder to hide.

I was recently called to a house that had been burgled and heavily vandalised. It was a detached house set in a large garden, and the owners were on a six-month business trip to the USA. They had taken some of the holiday countermeasures to disguise their absence but that wasn't enough. Unfortunately they hadn't identified the new problems presented by a longer absence. When they had been gone a couple of months, louts noticed that the house was clearly unoccupied, they broke in, stole some property and then stayed for at least an hour to trash the place. Toilets and basins were broken, taps were left on, paint thrown around and doors ripped off their hinges. The television was smashed and china and glassware was broken and thrown all over the house. The final bill for damage and loss ran into thousands of pounds.

Standing on the road outside the house, the signs and evidence that it was empty were clear and easy to see. For example:

- Tall weeds had grown up through the drive and around gates. Nobody was using the drive, car wheels and people's feet weren't knocking weeds down and killing them. Gates were not being opened, sweeping weeds aside. It was clear from casual observation that the drive and gates were not being used.
- It was late spring going into early summer, and bushes in the front garden had grown quickly, partly blocking the front path, the lounge windows and the front doorstep.
- Ivy that was growing up the side of the house had started growing across the living room window at the front of the house, a blatant sign that nobody was caring for the house.
- A telephone directory had been delivered and left on the front doorstep, but spring rain had begun to turn it into paper mulch.
- The front windows, front door and doorstep were all dirty and dusty. Even an untrained eye could clearly see that footprints in the dirt on the front step showed where a male (postman) had stood on the step then left. The footprints clearly showed that nobody had come out of the house.

Overall the impression was of an unloved and unused house. It didn't take a master detective to read the clues, even the brain dead local louts couldn't fail to notice – and unfortunately for the homeowner, they didn't.

Long holidays and business trips – countermeasures

If you are going to be gone for a long time, remember the lessons that can be learned from the case above. Spend some time identifying the new vulnerabilities to which you are exposed by being absent from your home for more than a couple of weeks. When you have identified them, define and introduce countermeasures to them. For example:

✔ If you are going away for more than three weeks, I suggest that you MUST have somebody trustworthy looking after your house, performing the duties listed above and below.
✔ Check your house insurance, as some policies are void if the house is empty for more than a specified number of weeks. You could find on return from an extended absence that your house has been destroyed but the insurance company refuses to pay out because the house had been left empty.
✔ Plan ahead and think of the seasons. Take time to consider the things that will happen while you are away and take steps to overcome any problems. For example:
  ➢ In **spring** – remember that plants put on a spurt of growth. In winter nothing much will happen in your garden, but during a three-week absence in a good spring, your garden can become a jungle. Hedges, ivy,

lawns, even weeds suddenly appear and demonstrate the lack of a controlling presence. Make sure that somebody is keeping an eye on the garden and trimming energetic plants back where needed.

➤ In **summer** – many plants put on a growth spurt, drought kills them, wasps and other pests build nests and take properties over. You should have arranged for somebody to be looking after the house and garden, and they should take whatever steps are necessary to keep everything in order. That may mean watering the lawn, or arranging for a wasps' nest to be removed from the porch!

➤ In **autumn** – the most noticeable difference is leaves falling from the trees. In itself that is not a major disaster, unless your garden is usually immaculate, then rafts of decaying leaves can display your absence. Add a little wind and the leaves can blow together to collect in sheltered corners which gives two problems. A stray bonfire night rocket can set fire to leaves collected against your shed or garage and put it at risk from fire. The same leaves can blow up against the back door, or collect on the front step, another clear sign that there is nobody home. Another job for the person watching the house: if the leaves are usually raked up and put on the compost pile, that is what should be done. They should certainly be looking for anything that is a clear sign of the absence of residents, such as making sure leaves don't collect on the front doorstep.

➤ In **winter** – frost and snow clearly show that there is no activity in a house. Activity leaves clearly visible tracks in heavy frost or snow, such as footprints, garage doors and gates being opened or closed, and car tyre track. If your house is the only one with none of these signs, your house is the one that will be noticed. If you are going on an extended holiday or business trip, you may have left your car in the garage. It may be beneficial for the person watching your house to start it up and take it for a run now and then to keep everything charged up and in good order as long as they are properly insured to use the vehicle. Occasionally using your car will be ideal because it will allow them to use the garage and leave wheel tracks in the snow and frost. Alternatively you could ask a neighbour to park their car in your drive so that there are signs of activity. After fresh snow, ask them to walk up and down the path a few times, break a path to the shed, make tracks out to the greenhouse, make it look as though there is some life at the house. Consider sweeping or shovelling snow off the drive and definitely clear any off the front doorstep!

✔ Make sure that somebody opens and closes the gates, and shed and garage doors. The opening action sweeps leaves and snow off the path showing that the doors and gates are in use.

✔ The person looking after the house should consider sweeping the path and drive; it will take some time but will show activity and occupation in a number of ways.

✔ The person looking after the house should keep an eye on the condition of windows and the front door and doorstep. They need to be swept, dusted and occasionally washed, or they can quickly look like vacant premises. Remember that there is no crime in walking up to a front door to ring the bell. A passing criminal could see a house that doesn't seem to be occupied and to check all they have to do is walk up and ring the front doorbell. If nobody answers, they make a note to come back when it is dark; if somebody answers they make excuses and leave.

✔ In the summer and autumn, the person looking after your house should be asked to check any fruit or vegetables growing in the garden. Ripening and uncollected fruit is suspicious. Tell the person looking after your house to collect and take any fruit or vegetables growing in the garden.

✔ At Christmas if you are away, you might ask the person looking after your house to put up a few decorations that are visible through the front window. Nothing elaborate is needed, just enough to show anyone who looks, that the phantom occupants are there and getting into the festive spirit by putting decorations up. Just as importantly, they must be taken down at the right time too!

✔ Increasingly properties need protection on Halloween. The American child's pastime of 'trick or treating' has been adopted by ever more louts. Their approach is more akin to blackmail and threats than childish fun. Any householder who does not answer their door and give food, money, drinks etc. to the louts is likely to suffer from blatant criminal acts. I have seen windows broken, cars vandalised, expensive shrubs broken off, paint thrown over a front door and fireworks pushed through letterboxes. If you plan to be away during Halloween it may be prudent to ask somebody to stay in the house and distribute a few pounds' worth of chocolate and fizzy drink cans to avoid trouble.

✔ You should also plan to avoid known local problems. Many areas suffer annual problems from a variety of large gatherings, be they pop festivals, large race meetings or other events that attract large numbers of people. If there is such an event in your area, and you can't plan your absence to be at home to protect your property at that time, you should certainly arrange for somebody to stay in the property over that period to protect it!

4　Neighbours

Everybody has neighbours. They may be inches away behind a party wall in a small row of terraced houses, above you in another high rise council flat, or in the next country mansion three miles away.

Neighbours can be other families or single people, office blocks, factories, churchyards, motorway junctions, a cinema or any number of other premises. The thing they all have in common is that they are located next to each other. They are there 365 days a year, 24 hours a day.

Neighbours and Security

From your house security survey you already know that different neighbours can have a different impact or influence on your security. We used an example of a semi-detached house that has a 24-hour petrol station as an immediate neighbour. The presence of that neighbour could be a security threat because it gives total strangers an excuse to be in the area near your house at any time of the day and night. Another example we used was of a badly managed public house at the end of a dead end road. Rowdy and drunken customers coming and going to that pub increase the security problems for every house in that road.

Neighbours can be a problem, but you must realise that neighbours can also enhance and improve your security. From old-fashioned community spirit with neighbourly concern for people living close by, to more formalised community watch systems, neighbours have co-operated to improve security in an area. For any of this to work, one thing is absolutely necessary, and that is to be on good terms with the neighbours.

Sociologists have written learned papers to describe the many forms of breakdown in modern society. There seems to be a lack of cohesion that leaves people not knowing the names of neighbours who have lived next to each other for years, or allows old folk to lie dead in their homes undiscovered and unmissed for weeks. Is it a breakdown in social relationships? Does that avoidance of relationships foster communities where you don't speak to or know the name of half of your neighbours?

Some experts have attributed it all to a modern fast-living world, where people don't think they have time to stop and speak to the people who live and work around them. Some say that with the increase in mobility people don't have time to get to know each other before they move on to another job or a new home. Others think that the increase of mindless crime is to blame, because people are basically too scared to get involved or to risk getting to know their neighbours. Whatever the reason is, it is clear that people are not talking to each other.

Local governments are now trying to rebuild links into fractured and disjointed communities. They are spending millions in building what they call 'community cohesion' in the hope that it will reduce crime and disorder, and hopefully banish anti-social behaviour.

But I believe that community cohesion will only work if it blooms naturally within the communities themselves, rather than being imposed or grafted on artificially. When people realise that they will benefit from any investment they make in their community they may make the effort, but they will only do that if they can clearly see that there will be a benefit to them!

One benefit is greater security. No matter who your neighbour is you will benefit from making contact with them, but not in a mercenary way. By making friends and expecting nothing, you will build relationships that will reward you in many ways.

Helpful neighbours

If you live next door to the 24-hour petrol station, at least in some part think of the staff there as 24-hour security guards. They will be as distrustful of you as you are of them, but over time a friendly nod will turn into a greeting. That greeting will become short conversations and before you know it you will be on friendly terms with them. Before that friendship was built, the garage employees would have ignored a stranger climbing over your side gate, but now they know you they are motivated to at least call the police to report unusual and suspicious behaviour. At the same time you might telephone the garage kiosk and ask if they knew that there are some lads climbing up on their storeroom roof, giving them the opportunity to check to see if it is just high spirits, or a prelude to stealing their tobacco supply. The same goes for any other neighbours, office employees, shop employees, school teachers and caretakers, or maybe just Mr and Mrs Biggins from number 42.

Neighbourly Disputes

All over the country people have allowed their relationship with their neighbours to deteriorate to a level where they end up in civil or criminal courts, disputing some legal point or other. Usually it isn't a deliberate act, it somehow seems to just 'happen'. Disputes between neighbours tend to start with a small or even insignificant issue. One side or both sides ignore it assuming it will go away, but a nugget of resentment can grow into a major conflict. The longer it remains unattended the larger it grows and the more acrimonious it all becomes.

I could understand how Mr and Mrs Average would want to take out an injunction against an illegal all-night drinking club that was set up in the house next door. However, I could never understand how relationships between two average families could break down to such a level about something as stupid as a hedge. With my experience I have seen how simple issues can deteriorate into full-scale hostilities and it always, always, always involves generous helpings of ego, arrogance, pride and a monumental lack of communication.

As an example of just such a dispute, as a police officer I was called to what we term a 'domestic dispute'. On arrival I found a younger man and a man who had taken early retirement rolling around on the front lawn of a house having a schoolboy style fight. We separated them and moved them apart to stop the dispute, then I spoke to the younger man and my colleague spoke to the older guy and we asked what had started the fight. After that we got together and compared the explanations.

- The young guy had said that he and his wife and son were trying to have a quiet life, but it was being ruined by the retired guy who was a miserable old devil, a killjoy who hated kids and wasn't happy unless he was complaining about something.
- The older guy had said the young family were anti-social, the young guy was a lout who didn't care about anyone other than himself and that he and his son were totally selfish and had absolutely no consideration for anyone but themselves.

Two strong and rather different views, but both men were absolutely certain that they were 100% right in what they were saying. Further discussion had disclosed the events that had caused them to form those opinions.

I tried to speak to them both but they were unwilling to listen to explanations, preferring to hurl abuse and accusations at each other. It was clear to me that the entire problem centred on a lack of understanding, which had been created by a communications blockage between them. Knowing what I knew after speaking to them both, I could see and, to an extent, understand both viewpoints. It was frustrating to me that compared to some calls I had to deal with this was all so ridiculous and was even worse because it had been brewing for at least seven months!

I got the two men back together, as from what I knew I thought they could resolve it if they only took time to sit and talk calmly over a cup of tea, but that suggestion was met with more anger and insults, only this time the wives joined in too. Unable and unwilling to waste more time on it I arrested both men and placed them in the back of the police van. I sat with them, while my colleague separated the wives who were now arguing and blaming each other for the arrest of their husbands.

In the back of the van I told both men to grow up and shut up while I described their problem, and then explained what was going to happen next in terms of cells and court appearances. As I described the problem as I saw it, one or the other would snort and give an 'I-told-you-so' gesture or look, and occasionally I had to shut them both up. This is what I told them.

When he was young the older guy had helped his father grow and show flowers in local competitions. His father died of cancer and the older guy had fallen into industrial work, where he worked long hours for low pay, living in a run-down city centre flat with no access to a garden. All his life he had wanted a garden so that he could again grow prize-winning flowers. When he became ill and was forced to give up work, the council moved them to a house with a small garden and it seemed to be an answer to his dreams.

When the younger family moved in next door, their son began 'carelessly' kicking balls around, damaging plants in the old guy's garden. Complaints seemed to be ignored and in fact, the older guy thought the boy's father was encouraging the boy to break plants. It all came to a head that weekend when prize competition blooms were snapped off by a stray football. Not wanting to ask for the return of the ball and no doubt taking a combative lead from his father's attitude to the neighbour and his flowers, the boy climbed the fence and retrieved his own ball. Unfortunately, in doing so he trampled more plants and was spotted by the older guy, which was the direct cause of the confrontation and fight on the front garden lawn that we had witnessed.

Having heard all of that, the younger guy looked a little sheepish, and the older guy looked triumphant. They both started talking but I told them both to shut up and listen, then I carried on.

The younger guy's son had fairly severe learning difficulties, and though he looked as though he was 12 years old, he had the mind of a child of six at best. Where they used to live the boy had been picked on, bullied and abused, making his parents desperate to protect him. The council had moved them to their current house, in a nice quiet neighbourhood where they hoped for a new start and a happy life for their son. Their peace didn't last long when the cranky old guy from next door began to endlessly complain about balls and flowers. The young guy thought the old guy next door was deliberately picking on his disabled son, because he was different!

When I finished it was time for the older guy to look sheepish. He managed to say 'I didn't know' then went quiet.

I de-arrested both of them and told them that now they had taken the time to explain their grievances and listen to the other side, they both understood what was causing the problems. I asked them to shake hands which they did quite readily, then I told them if I was called back they would be arrested again but this time they would be taken straight to custody and the courts. They left the van apologising to each other, lines of communication wide open and laying the foundations of understanding and friendship.

A few weeks later I was in the area and dropped in to see how things were. I found that the families were now the best of friends, the boy had taken to the old guy who was showing him how to grow flowers. He told me that the boy had a natural flair for gardening, and that growing the blooms he now understood why he should keep his ball off the flowers to prevent damage to them. If they had only taken time to talk in the first place, there would have been no fight and they could have avoided months of misery.

There are several routes that neighbourly disputes can take.

Solicitors

If a neighbourly dispute has reached the stage of involving solicitors it has not got out of control, it has been out of control for a long time. Consulting a solicitor will quickly achieve four things:

- It will help to make solicitors on both sides rich.
- It will escalate your dispute to a new level of bitterness and distress.
- It will complicate your dispute beyond recognition.
- Nobody will actually be happy when it is resolved.

If you have a problem, at least try to resolve it amicably yourself.

'Friendly' dispute resolution

We will use the example of the broken flowers above to illustrate the process. Disputes are almost always based on lack of information, misunderstanding and a breakdown of communications between the two parties. (In some cases, drug or drink problems and mental disorders cause or allow people to do things that are deliberately intended to aggravate neighbours. These cases are very rare.)

If a dispute or problem seems to be surfacing, talk it through with your neighbours as soon as you can. It may be carelessly parked cars, loud music, or apparently aggressive pet dogs. The earlier you address the problem, the smaller it is and the easier it will be to resolve it.

Talk to your neighbours

You should at least be talking to your neighbours, even if you are only asking if they have seen the postman yet or are jointly complaining about the weather. Though I accept that some people seem to adopt neighbours as honorary 'close family', constantly dropping in to each other's houses and discussing the most intimate details of their lives, you don't have to do that if you don't want to. Some people want to maintain what they see as their privacy and independence. They don't want to adopt an open door, walk-in-when-you-want-to policy. Either way, you build relationships, which involve as much trust and contact as close as you all want.

No matter what anyone might say, we don't live in isolation. We are inevitably part of our local community to some extent or other. As such, we should automatically and naturally build relationships with the people we come into contact with in that community, whether it is a 'best friend' relationship with the couple next door or just a nodding first names contact across the fence or supermarket trolley when you see them.

If you try to pretend they don't exist and ignore opportunities to at least say hello, they will assume that you are deliberately snubbing them. You might see it as simply an attempt not to get too closely involved, or perhaps a dignified way to maintain your distance and privacy. Unfortunately they probably see you as an arrogant, pretentious snob who thinks he or she is too good to talk to them. Though you were doing it innocently you might be planting the seeds of a nasty dispute that could make life a misery for you all. It doesn't take much to adopt a casual friendship. Offer to cut the lawn while they are on holiday, keep a watch on the house and maybe buy fresh bread and milk for them the day they are due back – it's as simple as that!

Simple courtesy is all that is required, with a touch of human warmth and natural concern. That approach will keep communications lines open, which makes it easier should you need to discuss a developing problem.

Resolving Neighbourly Disputes

Every case is different. Most people are normal and average just like you and me. They want a quiet life just as much as you do. I have proposed some steps below that should help you to resolve a dispute under normal circumstances. If you are the unlucky one in a million who does live next door to a drug crazed homicidal maniac you could still try these steps. If you do, make sure you are safe and be prepared to call the authorities before it escalates to violence.

Step 1 – Discuss the problem

Because you are (or should already be) on reasonably friendly terms with your neighbours you can at least speak to them. Be diplomatic when you approach them, and ask 'if they have time to help you with a little problem'.

Using the broken flower problem described above as our neighbourly dispute, I would expect the discussions and negotiations to progress along the lines of the description below.

The initial approach is important and sets the tone for the entire process. Be friendly and explain what the problem is in calm terms. Rather than say 'What the hell are you going to do about your delinquent kid wrecking my garden?', I would say something more like 'Could you spare a moment to help me work out how I can protect my flowers?'

If you used the 'delinquent' introduction, they are already on the defensive because you have attacked them, their child, as well as their upbringing and control of their child. The suggested 'protecting the flowers' approach has let them know that you have what you consider to be a problem, but you have not laid blame or confronted them. Everything is amicable and they agree to come round to talk.

Some people think that making that first conciliatory move is a sign of weakness, but I don't see it like that. I see it as a demonstration of maturity, good interpersonal skills and the first step to achieving your goal. After all, your objective is to stop your flowers getting damaged, not to lay blame, get revenge or impose punishment.

So the guy next door has agreed and is now following you into your garden. I would ask him in for a cup of tea, put the kettle on and sit them down while the kettle boils. During this period I would take the opportunity to show off my trophies and certificates that I have won over the years for my prize blooms.

By doing that I just smoothly achieved a number of things. I extended a conciliatory olive branch by inviting him in and making that tea. I have relaxed him, he isn't on the defensive. I have opened up to him – I am more of a person than just an unknown neighbour to him now. He now knows how important flowers are in my life and also knows that I grow prize-winning flowers for local shows. We chat a while about my trophies, and I give him an opportunity to boast about his car maintenance skills, pedigree cat or whatever else he passes his time with. He has finished his tea, it's time to move my mission forward.

'Here let me take your cup. Tell you what, come out into the garden and I'll show you my dahlias, I'm hoping to win a best in show this summer.'

He is still relaxed, no conflict yet. He might think I spend too much time with my dahlias, but so far he has no reason to dislike me let alone want to fight me. In the garden I show him my prize blooms, working round to the problem. At last we reach the broken plant with his son's footprints all around it.

'Ah this is it Colin,' (see, we are on first name terms now). 'This is the problem I was talking about. Look, I know kids like to play but I noticed your Sam came over to get his ball and accidentally stood on this plant.'

Colin is getting defensive now, I wasn't aggressive but he is beginning to think that I am accusing his one and only son and heir of murdering my prize blooms. Having spotted that coming I will immediately defuse the situation, remove the conflict, back away from accusations and give him a way of saving face in these circumstances.

'I'm lucky it wasn't one of my prize plants Colin,' (even if it was). 'Sam's a good lad and I know it was an accident but I was wondering if you could suggest a way I could protect these flowers – it's the big show in two weeks' time.'

No accusations have been made and there has so far been no excuse for any confrontation. By my saying that, he sees that I have pulled back from appearing to lay blame or make accusations. At the same time I have explained exactly what the problem is, shown him how serious it is to my lifestyle, and better still asked him for help in protecting my other plants and he is probably a little flattered that I need his help.

Step 2 – Look for a solution

Having drunk a cup of tea and chatted for 15 minutes, Colin is now fully aware of the problem as I see it, we are still on friendly terms and no accusations or confrontations have taken place. It's time for Colin to speak.

'Wow, will it recover?' He is showing concern, at the same time as finding out if the plant is dead or if it will recover given time.

'Yes, it'll come back, but it's these I'm worried about. Young Sam's got a good goal-scoring kick but my dahlias don't make very good goalies.'

I bought humour in to defuse any traces of tension that were building up, at the same time as praising young Sam. My neighbour can do one of three things now and they are:

- Kick a few more plants to death and jump over the fence telling me all the plants will be dead by next week (not likely).
- Promise to do something about it, go home and forget about it (again not likely now we are on friendly terms).
- Promise to do something about it and stay to discuss how we can protect the plants from that accidental kick (a win–win situation).

Under the circumstances, I suspect that he will adopt the third option and make genuine efforts to stop the ball from damaging my plants.

With the calm explanation and an absence of blame and accusations, we have done several things.

We made sure that the neighbour knows that:

- Flowers have been damaged (you just showed him).
- They aren't just flowers they are prize-winning blooms you have been raising for weeks.
- By growing them you have been working towards a particular and important flower show.
- You aren't laying blame, you are just looking for a solution.
- You are being open and offering friendship.

Step 3 – Implement the solution

You should now implement the agreed solution, while building on the neighbourly relationship.

Remember that you should not try to be too clever or manipulative, because that shows when you are dealing with people. If you try to manipulate people you will cause a conflict. The description above is not intended to be a lesson in manipulating your neighbours. It simply describes the approach I would take to avoid any appearance of confrontation or accusation.

Summary

- You should be talking to your neighbours and so be able to approach them to discuss any problems that occur (note I said discuss, not confront or accuse).
- Discuss any problems as soon as you can; the longer you leave it the worse it will get and the greater the effort needed to resolve it.
- Avoid laying blame and avoid any confrontation. The more amicable the discussion the more likely you are to agree on a solution that is acceptable to everyone.
- Be ready to compromise to achieve a solution.
- Don't see the solution as a victory, and don't gossip about the conflict. Because people gossip your neighbours might get to hear a twisted version of your description of the problem. For example, if the gossip has got round to Mrs Biggins she might be telling everyone that you are saying that Colin is so thick and spineless that it took you just two minutes to persuade him to put up a trellis on his side of the fence. Gossip you can live without, so keep any dispute, discussion, negotiation and agreement between the two of you. (If you hear any gossip about the dispute, accept that it is just gossip and don't get upset at the way it may have been exaggerated or twisted in the telling.)

Problem Log

Occasionally, for whatever reason, a dispute cannot be resolved over a cup of tea. On these rare occasions, you might have to escalate matters. What you do depends on you, the reason for the dispute and your situation. There are some things that you can still try. Allow things to cool off for a while, and then try again. Let your spouse talk to their spouse. Encourage your kids to play with their kids. Have a barbecue and invite a lot of neighbours including 'them'. Have a meeting on neutral territory – perhaps accidentally meet them in the supermarket. There are a number of things that you can try, but you will know when nothing is working.

At that time it may be appropriate to talk to the Citizens' Advice Bureau or maybe the local authority (especially if council tenants are involved). But if everything you try fails, you might end up in court, complaining to the housing association or council, or dealing with the police. If you do, you will need evidence and you will have to supply it. If your dispute ever reaches that stage, your evidence will have to cover an extended period, and will have to show an ongoing pattern of behaviour or activity that is evidenced over a period of months.

A complaint about constant noise cannot be upheld on the basis of one noisy New Year's party, or one occurrence of a neighbour working on a car engine early one Sunday morning. To support your grievance you will have to show that the problem (whatever it is) has been going on for weeks, if not months. The way you do that is to keep a log or diary detailing the incidents that are causing the problem. Any log should also include your attempts to defuse the situation. (Remember, if the neighbours become abusive or violent when you try to make peace and resolve the issue, you should withdraw.)

If for example you were suffering problems with a very noisy and aggressive neighbour, your log might look something like this.

Saturday 14th January

05:00 Party at number 34 broke up at five am. Lots of shouting in the street as guests departed revving their engines. John Smith tenant at number 34 thought it was funny and was shouting and laughing when he sounded his car horn continuously for two minutes.

06:45 Had only just got to sleep, woken by loud knocking on my front door. Went to find John Smith, very drunk demanding to know if I wanted a fight! I told him I didn't. He went away after five minutes called me a 'blooming chicken'.

08:12 Sandra Smith (wife of John at number 34) seen by Mr Simpson at number 27, throwing empty cans and broken bottles over fence onto my front lawn.

11:25 pm Arrived home to find windows of number 34 wide open, with extremely loud pop music playing. Neighbours complaining – somebody had called police. Police arrived, there was an argument at number 34, music shut off. Music put back on at even louder volume as soon as the police left.

11:58 pm Police came back, Mr Smith arrested, music turned off again following arrest.

Sunday 15th January

08:00 Woken by sound of breaking glass. Got up to see Mrs Smith from number 34 standing on my front lawn with a half brick in her hand, found another half brick in my lounge inside the broken window. Mrs Smith apparently drunk and shouting insults and claiming I had her husband arrested. I called police. Mrs Smith later arrested after assaulting police sergeant who attended.

Monday 16th January

08:30 Left house to drive to work but found all four car tyres slashed. I heard shouting, then saw Mr John Smith standing at his front door with craft knife, he was shouting 'Drive to work on them you rat.' I called police. Mr Smith arrested.

Tuesday 17th January

05:00 Woken by loud music. John Smith now has a loudspeaker and microphone. He was shouting at full volume over the loud music. Lights on all along the road with people complaining about the Smiths. Mr Smith shouting through the speaker 'Tom is a grass. Tom's a coward who lets the police do his fighting. Come out and fight you devil.' Smith had a wooden pole in his hand and I feared he would damage my car so I went out. I told him 'I don't want any trouble John, why don't you go and have a cup of tea and we can talk about this tomorrow.' He shouted 'You'll be dead by tomorrow.'

A man arrived and identified himself as William Jackson, council environmental health officer. He advised me to go indoors again. As I was going in through the door a car pulled up with excessively loud music playing and all windows open. The driver sounded his horn continuously. Police car drove up behind it (I later learned that they had been called by Mr Jackson), Billy Smith (son of John Smith) was arrested for drink driving. Mr Jackson advised John Smith to turn music down. John Smith refused, Jackson served a notice and Jackson seized the Smiths' music system with police support.

A rather extreme case, but all of this would be useful evidence of the problems you have had to suffer. It clearly proves that there wasn't one isolated incident such as a loud Christmas or family birthday party. I would suggest that you should aim to compile at least two months' worth of evidence in your log. While you are doing that, you could still try the other methods to find a resolution. Think back to the example used of the broken prize flowers, and try to identify a root cause to the conflict with your neighbours. Did you run their cat over, or do your kids break their flowers? If there is a root cause, make every effort to resolve it. If the matter cannot be resolved in a friendly manner and you have to report it to the authorities, you will already have a body of evidence that points to a persistent problem.

If you are not the only person suffering, I would suggest that you advise other neighbours to 'independently' compile their own log. Don't in any way conspire against an unpopular neighbour. Don't sit down at a residents' committee meeting and compile a neat collective log. Individual logs will be of more evidential value. Don't show each other your logs or discuss your entries. Just note what you have seen and heard.

For example, Mr Jones at number 1 could report a noisy session with motor-cycles that you knew nothing about because you were at work at the time. You might record some damage to your front fence that the people across the road know nothing about because they were out shopping at the time. The authorities will cross-reference all logs to see how extensive the problems are.

When compiling the logs only put in what you experienced, know, saw and heard. Don't be tempted to make things up so it looks better for your case. If the problem subsides for a few days, then so be it, you will have an empty page or two in the diary. When it starts up again you can carry on with the log.

Is it me?

When you have recorded a few weeks' worth of incidents, review your log. Take a step back and ask if it could possibly be you. Is there a chance that the only problem is that you are being particularly sensitive to something?

Review the log. If it contains a noisy party on December 24th (the Smith family Christmas party), then one on 14th February (the Smiths' wedding anniversary), you have to seriously sit and decide if for some reason you just don't like the Smiths and are looking for a reason to try to upset them. On the other hand if your log looks more like the example above, I think you are justified in taking it a stage further and asking the authorities to resolve the matter once and for all.

5 Bogus Callers

The hardest part of stealing valuables is getting into a house without being seen, finding the money or valuables and then getting out again without getting caught. Wouldn't it be good if a criminal could get you to invite him in, give him some time to look around and then show him out and wave goodbye? Good for him that is, not for you!

Unfortunately some criminals manage to do just that, and they use the bogus caller trick to arrange it. They claim to have some sort of official standing when they come to your door, trick you into letting them in, trick you into leaving them alone for a while, then they walk off with the family jewels or your life savings. This is sometimes called a 'distraction burglary'.

Distraction Burglary

It is easier to divert your attention if two or more of them work together. A pair of bogus callers will engage you in their trick – for example, a bogus meter reader will ask you to hold his torch while he gets in to write down the reading. Meanwhile his colleague who has been introduced as a trainee meter reader will ask if it is OK for him to use the toilet, which most people readily agree too. But you are trapped holding the torch in the hall while the meter reader pretends that his pen has broken and searches for another non-existent pen. He may even ask you to get a pen from the kitchen for him to use while his 'trainee' colleague is using the toilet – or in reality searching other rooms in the house.

This is a problem that could potentially affect anyone, though it is more likely to have more serious consequences for the elderly and infirm. Bogus callers take many forms, but they are all intent on a criminal objective. Some of the classic bogus caller tricks and methods are described below. The only effective counter-measure that is available to people is not to let the bogus callers into their home.

Statistics show that last year in the UK, 400,000 cases of bogus callers were reported. In at least 180,000 of those cases, the callers managed to get in and steal money or property. That sounds like a lot, but remember that unreported crime is generally thought to be at the very least, equal to reported crime. That means that the actual incidence of bogus callers was nearer 800,000 and about 360,000 people had things stolen by them. Personally I think that the level of distraction burglary is much higher!

This doesn't mean that the elderly are stupid, it simply reflects the fact that they were raised in a time when people were automatically deferential to anyone in authority. For them, somebody in what looks like a uniform would usually be trusted and obeyed without question. Today, there is a decreasing level of respect for authority figures and their argumentative attitude usually protects younger people from the same tricks. Nevertheless, everyone should be aware of the disguises and tricks that are used. Some common tricks are discussed below, but remember that anyone who comes to your door could be a bogus caller.

Bogus Meter Readers

Pretending to be an electricity or gas meter reader, the bogus caller knocks at your door. They appear to be wearing some sort of official uniform, with a clipboard and a friendly but slightly bored manner and ask where the meter is. Nobody really knows how often the meter reader calls, because they seem to come when they want to, and nobody is surprised to find one on their doorstep.

If they have done their research properly they will probably target elderly residents. They shine a torch, write something on a form clipped to their board, thank you and almost as an afterthought ask if they can use the toilet, or maybe ask for drink of water. Whatever they want, it is an excuse to get a chance to look around the house and pocket anything small and valuable. That done they thank the resident again and off they go. The loss is not likely to be discovered for some while, by which time they will be long gone.

Bogus meter reader – countermeasures

The countermeasures I advise to help you avoid becoming the victim to all bogus callers are similar and are listed below. I will not duplicate them for other versions of the bogus caller, but where there are different or extra considerations I will list them under the appropriate heading below.

- ✔ All officials carry some form of identification. If they arrive at your front door, you should ask to see their identification.
- ✔ If you have any doubts, there should be a phone number you can call to check the credentials of the man (or woman) on your doorstep.
- ✔ Caution: if the suspect caller gives you a phone number to call to check up on them, they might just give you the number of a crooked accomplice who will of course vouch for them. If you have any doubts, get a number for the gas company or electricity company they claim to represent from the telephone book, your last gas or electricity bill or directory enquiries and make an independent check on the caller.
- ✔ If the caller is genuine, they will not mind waiting outside the front door for you to confirm their identity.
- ✔ Fit and use a door chain – that is, a chain that allows the door to be opened enough to see and talk to callers but which will prevent them from easily pushing their way in. Even if they threaten you and demand that you open the door, they know you can't take the chain off without closing the door first. If you are suspicious or unhappy about a caller, you should close the door and immediately call the police, ask for assistance then wait for the police to arrive. Do NOT open the door again unless it is a police officer knocking. Confirm that by looking out of the window for a police car and real police uniform.
- ✔ If you do allow a caller into your home, never leave them unattended, whoever they are! Always make sure that you stay in the room with them, and if you have any doubts as to their activities ask them to leave. If your meter reader does say he has a trainee with him, you can always politely ask the trainee to stay outside, and if they are genuine they will not object.
- ✔ If you are expecting a meter reader, plumber or any other caller, make sure that you don't put unnecessary temptations before them. Put cash and credit cards away. Put handbags and wallets somewhere out of sight where they will have no need to go. Put small valuables such as jewellery, watches, mobile phones and so on out of sight and in a place where they have no need to go. This isn't an insult to the caller, you are simply avoiding mistakes and misunderstandings.
- ✔ If you have *any suspicions*, don't let them in and call the police and explain the circumstances. They will check with the company or authority to see if they have staff in the area, and if resources allow they will dispatch a police officer to check that caller out.

✔ The blind or disabled can usually arrange for a meter reader to come by appointment, when you could have a relative or carer with you to make sure the meter reader can get in and that they only read the meter while they are there.

Bogus Council Employees

This is the same trick but using a different excuse. The caller claims to be from the local authority or housing association. They spin a story about checking the property prior to redecoration, replacement of the gutters or a check on the status of the back garden.

The excuse is to get them in through the front door. Once there they adopt the usual routine of engaging the householder in their tricks. For example, the householder is asked to show one guy through to the back gutters while his colleague says he will check the front. Once in the garden the criminal will distract the householder, asking about the flowers, pointing out problems with neighbour's gutters, or getting you to hold the clipboard while he tugs at the fence to see how strong it is. Copious compliments on the quality of the garden and the tidiness of the house all keep your attention away from the other criminal who has already done a tidy search of the lounge and kitchen and is now upstairs going through the bedrooms.

The one talking to you won't finish his task until the second man appears to report that the front gutters are OK. His praise for the state of the house, garden or gutters raises a smile on the face of the resident and tells our criminal that his colleague has finished checking the house and has stolen everything worth taking.

Once again, they smile and go on their way to try the same trick at a few other houses in the street, before they think they have pushed their luck too far and move on.

Bogus council employees – countermeasures

As above, plus:

✔ Genuine council employees usually have recognisable uniforms.
✔ Genuine council employees usually make appointments with householders.

✔ Genuine council employees usually drive distinctive vehicles in council livery – council colours, with council crests painted on the sides. If in doubt call the council BEFORE you let them in!

✔ If you can't get through to the council, call the police and explain your concerns.

Bogus Travellers in Distress

There are many different versions of this trick. For example, a couple of nice clean young men claim their car has broken down nearby. They say they need to use a phone because they are on their way to visit their mum who is in hospital following an accident. On the other hand it could be a group of ten-year-old children, (yes, even young kids can be criminals too), telling you they lost their puppy and saw it run in through your gate and asking if they can look for it.

Their aims are the same, to engage you in their tricks and engineer an opportunity to take a look around and steal as much as they can. One of the young men uses the phone and the other may ask if he can use the toilet, or ask you to get pen and paper so they can write a note to leave in the car, or anything else they can think of to distract you while they find what they can take. With the kids and their stray puppy, they will probably ask you to help look for it, but while the kids are milling around, you lose track of them and don't realise that one or two of them have slipped off to search the house.

Bogus travellers in distress – countermeasures

As above, plus:

✔ You don't have to open the door to bogus travellers, or genuine ones for that matter – keep the door chain on!

✔ If somebody has broken down and you want to assist them you can ask them to push their AA or RAC membership card through the letterbox and you will make the telephone call for them. A genuine traveller should have no objection to that. A bogus traveller could pass you a stolen membership card, but it gets him nothing because he is still outside, and you have a card with his fingerprints on it!

✔ If anyone wants to search your garden for a lost puppy you can agree or simply tell them no they can't, then tell them that you are calling the police and watch them run off.

✔ If you do scare bogus callers away, call the police anyway and warn them that thieves are operating in the area so nobody else gets caught out.

Bogus Workmen

Cowboy workmen often try to trick their way into homes, but their tricks have some additional ploys built in. They will try to trick their way into your home to steal things, but they have added some refinements, which usually revolve around them telling you that you need urgent building repairs. For example, they claim that while they were passing they saw that a slate on the roof was cracked. They then try to frighten you, especially if you are elderly, by claiming that if the tile isn't replaced immediately the roof will rot away or fall off.

If they can persuade you to agree to have the work done, the 'builders', who are conveniently travelling in a lorry with ladders and slates and other materials, will climb up onto the roof. They usually fiddle around for half an hour or so and then come down, claim to have fixed the problem and demand an extortionate fee. They have even been known to take an elderly householder to a cash point or bank so that they can draw out money to pay them.

Otherwise they can ask to go inside the house to look out of the bedroom windows or check inside the loft for water damage. Once inside, of course they help themselves to anything they can, while you are distracted.

Bogus workmen – countermeasures

As above, plus:

✔ Never listen to a door-to-door salesperson, builder, gardener or anyone. If you have not asked them to call on you, tell them no thanks and ask them to leave. If they show the slightest hesitation call the police.

✔ If you do need work done ask friends, family and neighbours to recommend a reliable, trustworthy tradesperson who does good work for a fair price.

✔ Ask at least three genuine tradespeople to give you a quote on the work. Tell them you are getting three quotes. Make an appointment for them to come and do the quote. When they come make sure all tempting valuables are out of sight. Never leave them alone when they are in the house.

✔ Make sure that the builder has a known company name and address. A lot of cowboy tradespeople advertise with just a mobile phone number for a contact. As you can buy a mobile phone quite easily, if something goes wrong with your job, you won't get far if all you know about the builder is he called himself John and gave a mobile phone number that is now unobtainable! Get a name and address, recommendations, and even visit his address to see if he is actually there!

✔ When you get a quote for some work, ask if there is any additional fee. Some quotes do not include VAT, or materials, design services or arrangements for council planning permission, etc. What you are looking for is an all in price.

✔ When you get a quote ask for a definite schedule for the work. A vague 'should take a couple of days and I think I can start next week' will not be acceptable to me. I want something more like 'It's two and a half days work, and I can start on Monday the 15th. Allowing for the first coat of paint to dry, I will have finished the job by five o'clock on the afternoon of Thursday the 18th.'

✔ When you are close to accepting a quote, ask for some references. Preferably people you know, or people who live close enough for you to at least go and see if they exist, and who will even show you the quality of the work that builder produces and tell you how happy they were with the job.

✔ NEVER pay until the job is completed and you are absolutely and completely happy that the work is completed and that they have done a good job.

✔ If a builder or other tradesperson asks you for money up front to buy materials for your job, wave goodbye. Get somebody else to do the work. I accept that some smaller builders may have a cash flow problem and need you to pay for materials in advance of the job, but too many cowboys use that as a trick to part you from your money. For that reason I will not use a worker who wants any money in advance.

Bogus Salespeople

Bogus salespeople are a double risk. They could talk their way into your home to steal things, but their crime may be to get you to buy something worthless or which they have no intention of delivering.

Bogus sales people – countermeasures

As above, plus:

✔ Never buy anything at the front door – no matter how much of a bargain they may make it sound, no matter how much pressure they might put on you by telling you it is a limited offer or the last one, etc. If you say it is too expensive or that you couldn't afford to buy it until next month and they suddenly say they can reduce the price further or extend the deadline – wave goodbye, they are dishonest tricksters.

✔ Remember sales people are practised in getting your sympathy, it's part of their sales technique. For example a) telling you they still have 35 calls to make, b) they have a bad ankle, c) it's coming on to rain, d) they'll get the sack if they don't make at least one sale today. There are a million lines that they can use, and they will use them. Don't fall for their stories and never be sympathetic.

✔ Some salespeople – even those from reputable companies – rely on wearing you down. When they get into your house you won't be able to get rid of them, they insist on showing you just one more feature, they make a call to their area manager to get 'special permission' to give you another 2% discount, they offer free installation and delivery. They will find excuse after excuse to stay. When you have had enough, be blunt, be rude if you have to, tell them they are no longer welcome and tell them to leave. If they don't, call the police!

✔ The best countermeasure of all is not to let them in. Don't open the door, or if you do, keep the chain on. Ask what they want and unless you have actually asked for them to come don't let them start their sales pitch. Tell them no thanks and shut the door. If they ring again, shout through the door that you are calling the police to get rid of them. If they don't go – call the police.

General Advice
■ ■

No matter what they pretend to be, they want to get inside your house and distract your while they steal money or valuables. Stay alert and stop them from targeting you or others in your area.

Bogus callers – countermeasures

As above, plus:

✔ Keep the phone number of the local police at hand. If you suspect that bogus caller criminals are operating in the area, report them before they have a chance to steal from vulnerable people nearby.

✔ If you live near any elderly or infirm people, be neighbourly. If you see somebody on their doorstep, especially if they appear to be trying to talk their way in, take the time to drop by and say hello to your neighbour. They may introduce you to their nephew 'Hank' from America, or they may be glad of the support to get rid of a persistent double glazing salesman who won't take no for an answer, or it might just be a criminal trying his luck!

✔ If you do see suspicious activity in your street, YOU should call the police and report your suspicions, even if the people you are reporting have not tried to target you. Assuming there is no major incident and the police have resources available to deploy to the incident, they will be happy to come and check out the characters knocking on the doors of all the elderly people in the area.

✔ Be aware that some fittings and fixtures could indicate that a resident is infirm and or vulnerable, which will make them more likely to be targeted by the bogus caller criminal. Handrails, wheelchair access ramps or perhaps an electric wheelchair garage and charging point outside a house indicate that at least one resident is disabled or infirm. Similarly a substantial house (which indicates a level of wealth and presence of valuables) combined with an overgrown garden and poor house maintenance could indicate an infirm, disabled or elderly resident.

✔ If you report somebody, remember to give appropriate details. See Chapter 6 for more guidance.

6 If the Worst Happens

There are criminals out there. Crime happens – no matter how careful you are you could be unlucky and find that you are the victim of some crime or other.

What should you do and why would you do it? The advice below should help.

Reporting Incidents to the Police

If you do have to make a telephone call about a suspicious caller, be ready to give as good a description as you can. If all you can report is 'A guy with black hair', don't expect the police to find him. The police need to know who to look out for. Your description of a guy with black hair is of little or no use, but at least the police can exclude females from their search!

The police may well want to find and detain your suspicious character to talk to him, so they really want to know who to look for while they are driving around or checking via CCTV cameras in the town. For those purposes they need some easy identifiers. If your description of the suspect was white male, six foot six inches tall, shaved head, white trousers and a dark blue jumper, they have something to work on. Knowing that they can ignore anyone with hair, anyone who is short, any women and children, etc. They can more easily keep an eye out for very tall bald guys with white trousers and dark blue jumper.

When they find him they may want further details to confirm they have the right man, so the rest of your description will be invaluable. The rest of your description might include the fact that he spoke with a Welsh accent and that there was a little red crest on the left breast of his jumper. The man you saw also had nicotine stains on the fingers of his left hand, a snake tattoo on the back of his right hand and he presented what looked like a home-made gas company identity card stating he was Frank James – District Assessor.

That should give the police plenty to work on. If Mr Frank James really is the

District Assessor with the local gas company he won't mind you being careful. If he isn't, he will wish he hadn't come to your door!

As with any similar matters, when you have to report matters to the police, as soon as possible after the encounter write down as much as you can while it is fresh in your mind. That way, names, car registration numbers and other such detail don't get lost or confused.

Descriptions

Depending on the circumstances a full description for each person involved would include as much of the following as possible:

- sex
- age
- height
- weight/build
- race/colour
- hair colour/length/style/ornaments, etc.
- clothing/style/colour/markings, etc.
- jewellery
- identifying marks – tattoos/birth marks/scars, etc.
- voice/accent/impediment (stutter)
- names used – called himself Frank James, or colleague called him 'Barry', etc.
- anything carried – bag/briefcase/clipboard
- other identifying features, e.g. limp on left leg
- what he said – e.g. Claimed to be charity collector
- what they touched/ate/drank, etc.
- anyone else in the area who could give an independent description to police – e.g. 'He called on Mrs Biggins at number 42 before he came to me'
- if they had a vehicle:
  - make
  - model
  - colour
  - age
  - registration number or partial number if that's all you saw
  - markings, e.g. 'Grabbit & Scarper – Builders' in black lettering on side of light blue van – no phone number shown
  - other identifying features, e.g. rusty roof rack, broken left headlight, etc.
  - direction of travel if it has left the scene, e.g. they turned left onto the A40 heading into town.

The more detail you can supply, the easier you make it for the police to track down the culprit. If you are a witness to any crime, you should be using your powers of observation and filing details away in your memory so that you can accurately report them later.

Report immediately

As soon as it is practical you should report any crime to the authorities, with as much detail as possible. If you report crimes quickly, the criminals will still be in the area, they may still be carrying the proceeds of the crime, they will be wearing the same clothes and probably will still be with any accomplices, all of which makes them easier to spot. The longer you wait to report the crime, the harder it gets, as they will have left the area, changed clothes and passed on incriminating items, giving the police less grounds to stop and detain them.

Tell the police about any evidence

When you report crimes, ask if somebody will be coming to look for fingerprints or other evidence. Tell the police what you have found. If they say they will be sending somebody, ask when they will come, because you don't want to leave broken glass in the kitchen for a week. If they are delayed and if the guy touched your kettle tell them you want to use it because you are desperate for a cup of tea! If a window was broken and the guy touched the broken glass or cut his hand and left blood on the glass tell the police. If it's raining or there's thick fog or the conditions are frosty it may erase evidence, so you may want to explain to the police that there is broken glass with blood on it in the flowerbed under the window and that it is starting to rain. The police may advise you to protect or retrieve that evidence for them, but only touch things if the police tell you to or say it is OK and then only do what you are told.

If they say an expert will be visiting you but that will be at some time after the weekend, or in the next two days, explain your circumstances. For example, you could tell them that in order to shut the back door you will have to tidy up, or perhaps that you need to tidy the bedroom so you can go to bed. Maybe you will have to get a window boarded up or repaired because the criminal broke it, whatever the circumstances explain them to the police.

Imagine, for example, that you have been visited by a bogus council inspector and now realise that an antique gold pocket watch has gone missing. You call the police and pass on as much detail as you can, so that they can start looking for the thief and they tell you an officer will come around to fill in a crime report. Is there anything else that you can do? The answer is yes, quite a bit actually: protect, record, search and detail:

Protect

The police will probably send a fingerprint expert around to look at the premises. If you were there, and you know what the criminal touched, so you should make a note of that, and protect any surfaces that may still contain his fingerprints. The criminal may have asked for a glass of water, or taken a bite out of a biscuit while he was there. Anything he touched should be protected for the fingerprint experts to look at.

Record

The police are often very busy, which means that there may be nobody free to talk to you until later that day. For that reason I always suggest that victims should sit and write down as much as they can remember while it is fresh in their mind. Record the age, sex, height, etc. of the offender, but also try to make a quick note of what he did from the time he came in to the time he left. What did he say? What did he touch? Did he sneeze into a tissue that he threw into the bin? Make a little note of everything, before you forget. If he touched anything, DON'T touch it until the police have had a chance to look at it. If he emptied the contents of the desk drawers onto the living room carpet, no matter how tempting it is to pick it all up, leave it there for the police to see. They have skills and experience that you don't have, and while there may be no clues in the untidy heap on the living room carpet, if there are any clues there you don't want to lose them by being tidy!

If the criminal left by the back door then walked through the flowerbed and jumped over the back fence, take a look. If there is a set of his footprints in the rose border, point them out to the police when they come. If it is coming on to rain and you don't know when the police will arrive, consider protecting the footprints if you can. A dustbin lid or a sheet of plastic will protect the print from the rain, as long as you are careful not to damage the prints while you are doing it.

Search

You have given the police as much information about the criminal as you can. You have told him that grandfather's antique gold pocket watch is missing, but is that all? You noticed the watch was missing but did the criminal take anything else? If you can do so without disturbing evidence, you should check to see if anything else is missing. Is grandmother's Edwardian diamond necklace still in its box in the top drawer? Stop to think. Where did the criminal go, what did he have access to? If he didn't go near the back bedroom, your savings in the wardrobe are safe. He was alone in the kitchen for a while, did he find the bank books and credit cards in your handbag? Did he get the money in the cash tin that you keep behind the blue glass vase in the kitchen cupboard?

Think about where he went in the house, what he had access to and what he may have taken. Carefully take a look to see if there is something else he has taken and make a note of it. Also make a note that to get to that cash box, for example, he would have had to open the cupboard door and move the blue glass vase to get to it.

Remember, – don't destroy any evidence. By opening the cash box you could rub out his fingerprints. Using the example of the cash box behind the blue glass vase in the kitchen cupboard, let us explore further and see how we can protect any possible evidence by being careful. A long serving inspector once told me the most important thing to do when searching is to stop, stand back and search with your eyes first! Don't rush in and move everything, stand at the door and look at the evidence in front of you. By taking the time to do that you should know where the critical and valuable evidence is before you even step into the room.

So we have called the police and are awaiting an officer. In the meantime we are protecting the things we know the criminal touched but are looking to see if there is anything else missing. In the kitchen we can't see any signs that anyone touched the cupboards, but just in case we open the doors without touching the plastic handles! The first two only contain food and pots and they haven't been disturbed, the last cupboard has our cash box so we take extra care with that. Again we open the door without touching the plastic handle, and inside we can see that the glass vase has been moved and that the cash box lid is half open.

DON'T TOUCH ANYTHING. It is likely that the vase and the cash box and maybe the contents of the cash box have fingerprints on them and if we go any further we may smudge them. Make a note so that when the police come we can tell them that it looks like the criminal moved the vase, opened the cash box, then put the box and the vase back in the cupboard – the fingerprint expert will want to take a look at that!

Details

We have protected evidence, recorded what we know so we don't forget anything, searched to see if anything else is missing while being careful not to damage or remove any evidence the criminal left. The last thing we can do is to prepare details.

We knew that grandfather's antique gold watch is missing and following the search we know that the digital camera has gone too. Because we are security minded we have more detail than that, so we search our records, then when the police arrive we can give them details. We can give them the exact details of the gold watch, a recent valuation, a photo with a scale on it, and the wording of the engraving inside the watch case. We can also give the police the make, model and serial number of the digital camera that has been taken. More than that we can say it was in a black leather case, and the photographs held in its memory feature Aunt Mary and crowds on the beach at Brighton on a sunny day.

With all of that information the police will be pleased to speak to somebody who is so organised and security conscious. It will make a change from the victims who can barely remember what was taken, let alone what the make, model and serial numbers were.

Discovering an Intruder

Though most burglars will not attack a house if there are people at home, people have been known to wake at night or hear noises in other rooms during the day. If an intruder has entered your house, they will want to get away as soon as they can. They will not want to come face to face with you.

It is suggested that you should NOT attempt to challenge, detain or capture an intruder. You do not know what state of mind they are in. You do not know if they are under the influence of drugs. Perhaps they would be scared enough to use the screwdriver they used to break the window open as a weapon. There are dozens of arguments against tackling an intruder, so let them go.

Discovering an intruder – countermeasures

✔ Don't try to catch them or see them.

✔ Make as much noise as you can. Shout, use a mobile phone to call the police or loudly pretend to call the police – the burglar won't know – rattle doors and make a noise. If anyone is there, they will hear the noises and run. (Remember the first thing a burglar usually does when he enters any premises is to secure his exit route. He might have the front door or back door open, whatever his route is it will be clear for him to use.)

✔ At the first sign of disturbance they will run and you will be safe.

✔ Prepare to be a little embarrassed. Nine times out of ten, that 'late night intruder' is going to be the cat knocking an ornament over, water pipes creaking or somebody going to the toilet. With teenage kids, the intruder is usually one of them trying to sneak in very, very late to avoid answering your 'where have you been until this hour' demands!

Coming Home to an Intruder

Very rarely, a householder will come home and find that the front door is open, and even more rarely, there is somebody moving around upstairs using a torch to search for valuables.

Again, the best advice is not to challenge them. Even if you are a rugby team sharing a house, you don't know who is in the building and what weapons they may have. Quietly move to safety and call the police.

Coming home to an intruder – countermeasures

✔ Don't disturb them or warn them of your presence.

✔ Stay back and out of sight if you can, and use a mobile phone to report the problem to the police.

✔ Be careful to explain that you have disturbed intruders on the premises, and that they are still on the premises.

✔ If you have any additional information, pass it on. For example, you may have seen at least two people in the house, or there may be a strange white van parked outside your house. Give all the information you have to the police. If you are using a mobile phone, try to stay on the line to give a commentary on what is happening. For example, if while you were watching and before the police arrived, two men left your house, you could give a description of the men, what they are wearing, what they are carrying and which way they went. All of this would give the police more chance of catching the criminals.

Get a Police Crime Reference Number

When you report a crime to the police they usually take the details and give you a reference number that relates to that crime report, but they may call it something different. If they give you a crime reference number make a note of it because you will need it. If they don't give you a reference number ask for one.

After a Burglary

Following the 'protect, record, search, detail' procedure, protect the rest of your valuables and any evidence there may be. Record everything you know as soon as you can, as by tomorrow you might have forgotten the registration number of the van the burglar used! Search as far as you can without disturbing evidence to see what else has been disturbed and/or taken. Produce as much detail as you can for the police – make, model, serial number, photographs, etc. will all be very helpful in tracing the property and identifying the criminal.

Report and Make Insurance Claim

Assuming you have insurance, you should contact the insurance company to report the crime and to ask for appropriate claim forms to be sent to you. If you make a claim, report the details of everything that has been lost, but note that other things may be missing which you have not yet missed.

Most insurance claims require you to give them the crime reference number, which the police gave to you when you reported the crime. Without that crime reference number they may not allow you to make a claim – which means if you don't report it to the police you won't be able to claim on your insurance.

Investigate and Resolve Vulnerability

Because you have been the victim of crime, perform an urgent security review of the property, concentrating on the point of weakness where the intruder gained access. There may not be a weakness, the criminal may, for example, have smashed the patio doors with a slab of concrete to gain access. If they did there is little you can do to prevent that sort of attack (although in that example you could have removed the old broken slabs so the criminal had nothing to use to break the patio windows).

Perhaps when you hired Mrs Biggins to clean the house for you every Thursday, you failed to check her references. Perhaps the Mrs Jones she claimed she cleaned for without a problem for ten years doesn't exist, or perhaps she does and she sacked Mrs Biggins for taking money from the house.

Whatever the vulnerability, threat or risk, review it now and urgently implement countermeasures where possible to prevent any further loss.

When you do so, remember not to make your house too secure. Sometimes there is a backlash against becoming a victim, which makes people introduce ultra security, triple locking and bolting all of the doors and putting steel bars on the windows. Remember that if there is a fire or other emergency you want to be able to get out in a hurry, so only take reasonable countermeasures.

Make It Your Home Again

Don't underestimate the impact a crime can have on the victim. Home is your private domain, a place where you can relax and feel safe. To many people a burglary or other criminal intrusion damages or destroys that feeling of safety and security. In their mind the home feels corrupted and sullied because the criminal has violated their sanctity.

Happy family memories have been overwritten so the whole house now contains memories of that intrusion. Every time the homeowner uses the stairs they see in their mind the burglar creeping up and down those stairs. When they go into the bedroom, in their mind's eye they see the criminal searching through the dressing table and taking their jewellery.

This feeling that the home is just a building now, that the safety and comfort factor has been removed, that the feeling of peace has been corrupted, is more usual and often stronger among women than it is among men. Men do feel the same things but either they hide it, suppress it or get over it more quickly than women do.

That 'bad feeling' in the house often causes a lot of additional and ongoing stress to the residents after the crime. It does fade over time, but I have known people to sell up and move house because they cannot abide the memories of the intrusion and violation they feel their life has suffered at the hands of a criminal.

If it helps, I am told that those feelings can be erased, overwritten, washed away or counterbalanced with 'good memories'. The victims of intruder crimes have found that the following measures have helped to make their house feel like home again.

Fix the problem

As stated above your first and most important action is to fix the problem. Find out how the criminal bypassed or overcame your security and introduce new countermeasures to stop anyone else doing the same thing. You will sleep easier knowing that your security is tight once again.

Refresh or remove

Where possible and where you can afford to do so, dispose of anything that has been sullied by the touch of the criminal. I remember one lady was distraught that a burglar had rummaged through her underwear drawer looking for valuables, and refused to wear any of her clothes again. You can buy new clothes (send any unwanted clothes to the charity shop). If furniture is involved, you can swap a 'tainted' dressing table with a similar one at a second-hand shop for a minimal fee, or swap it with Aunt Mary for free!

For curtains and bedding, you may be able to swap them with relatives, so that those 'contaminated' by the intruder will be removed and 'safe' bedding and curtains can be put up in their place. It may be possible to recover something that was corrupted by an intruder – for example, have the carpets professionally cleaned to remove all traces of the villain. The basic rule is to take any steps you can to refresh the home.

Decorate

Decorating can help. The smell of fresh paint, somehow masks and removes the 'smell' and feel of the criminal's presence. Giving the house a makeover and fresh new look helps as well, by distancing the current home from the home that was violated by an uncaring intruder. For most women a home makeover is overdue the day after you finish decorating anyway!

Party

When you have taken as many of the above steps as are practical to remove traces of the intruder, you should have a party. Invite as many good friends and relatives as you can. Warn them that any discussion, mention of or questions about the crime will destroy what you have been trying to do. Do everything you can to make it the happiest party ever. The party will then flood the new look home with new happy memories revolving around friends, fun and a good time.

Start again

One lady I know of was so traumatised by the intrusion into her home that she wanted to sell up and move out. Her husband suggested that she go to stay with their daughter for a holiday. While she was away, he installed new door and window locks, a burglar alarm and passive sensor operated lighting on the sides and rear of the house, decorated throughout and upgraded the kitchen. When she came back she said it was like coming into a new house, and they threw a big party to celebrate their 'new' house.

Hopefully all of those actions will make the home feel like a safe shelter from the world again. Remember to still be sensitive to the feelings of anyone badly affected by an intruder. Try not to mention it or anything to do with it. Try to build on the feeling of peace and security that person has. If they want to be quiet, let them. If they want to search for new super strength door locks, help them. Do anything you can to help that person rebuild the feeling of security that they need.

7 Next Steps

■ ■

What should you do when you have completed your survey? You may be the world's greatest administrator, or you may get confused if you have more than one task to perform. This chapter suggests a simple approach to selecting, documenting and implementing your chosen countermeasures.

Already Started
■ ■

If you took my advice, you have probably already started responding to and resolving any problems that you identified during your survey. You must now begin a formal process that will allow you to manage and resolve the problems you found and listed by implementing the selected countermeasures.

Identifying security issues

During the survey you may have simply listed the security problems you encountered, or you may have written pages of notes. Somewhere you should also have listed possible countermeasures associated with each problem.

Some countermeasures were easy and simple to do, so you have already introduced them. For example, you may already have cut back overgrown bushes and be shutting that window when you leave, so Tiddles the cat will have to wait outside until you come home.

Other countermeasures are awaiting your attention, but first you must decide what to implement and how to do it.

List Problems and Countermeasures

You should start by looking back through the notes and lists you have written and draw up a tidy list of all vulnerabilities, risks and threats that you have identified. For simplicity I will call them 'problems'.

Against each problem, you should list any known or potential countermeasures that you have identified. At this stage, you may have identified a problem for which you cannot identify a workable countermeasure. That is acceptable; simply list the problem with no proposed countermeasure.

When you have finished, you will at least have documented all of the problems that you identified, so you will not lose track of them.

The problems you identify may be quite lengthy, for example 'Front door swells up and sticks in winter, but dries out and shrinks in summer making the front door loose and insecure'. For that reason you should assign a number and key word to each problem for ease of reference. See the example below.

Ref No	Key Word	Problem	Countermeasure	Priority
SR1/1	Porch	It is possible for intruders to hide in porch alcove	Fit door viewer in front door and fit light on porch	
SR1/2	Front door	Front door swells up and sticks in winter, but dries out and shrinks in summer making the front door loose and insecure	Fit new door and frame with security equipment identified in SR1/3, SR1/4 and SR1/5 below	
SR1/3	Front door	Letter box unprotected	Fit draught excluder and mail basket inside letter box	
SR1/4	Front door	No hinge bolts on front door	Fit hinge bolts	
SR1/5	Front door	No approved mortice lock on front door	Fit approved mortice locks	

Identify and select countermeasures

Against some problems you will have listed several possible countermeasures, while against others there may be only one, or even no proposed countermeasures. You should now invest some time in researching those countermeasures, so that you can select, nominate and list those countermeasures that you are going to implement. You may need to:

- Seek expert advice from a tradesperson – what locks would be best suited for use on a patio or garage door?
- Investigate the need for planning permission from the local authority to erect a wall or high fence.
- Seek permission for structural changes from your landlord.
- Look into the availability and cost of new fixtures and fitting.
- Investigate the availability, time, skills, tools and costs involved with implementing any particular countermeasure.
- Ask for advice from the local police crime prevention officer, who may be able to suggest countermeasures where you have been unable to identify any.

All of the above actions should help you to review the problems and the effort needed to implement a potential countermeasure. That should then allow you to compare them, and to select the countermeasure that you want to introduce to improve your security.

Your final objective is to draw up a list of all identified problems and the countermeasures you propose to introduce to overcome those problems.

Establish countermeasure priority

When you have finished listing the countermeasures you plan to introduce, you should assign priorities to them. This will be easier using a computer, because you will be able easily to change the order by cutting and pasting. If you don't have a computer available you may want to do it using sticky notes. As some people don't have a computer available I will assume you are using sticky notes, which you will stick to flip chart pages (or the wall if you have to) to sort and organise your countermeasures.

I suggest that you assign your problems and countermeasures under four headings:

- (I) Immediate
- (S) Soon

- (I & W) If and when possible
- (NS) Non-security.

You should write the reference number and key word of each problem and the countermeasures on a new sticky note and add it to the appropriate list. Thus you might write 'SR1/1 Porch – fit porch light' and on another note 'SR1/1 Porch – Fit door viewer'. Using the reference number and key word makes the task manageable, and what is written on the sticky note is enough to remind you what it is actually about.

Your perception of the priority, time required, cost, skills, impact and benefit will eventually allow you to produce a final countermeasure priority list. Remember that the priority rating will be a combination of factors. The most important of these are:

- The **threat or risk** that the countermeasure will remove or protect against. For example, a rotten front door to which you have lost two keys that had an address tag on them is a major concern. The threat and risk is that the door is no longer secure at all.
- The **time** required to implement the countermeasure. For example, it will take about half a day to replace the front door. John the carpenter is good and reliable so it will be half a day well spent.
- The **cost** of implementing the countermeasure. Though a total cost of £418 is quite expensive, a secure front door is so fundamental to the security of the house that it must be done as soon as possible.
- **Skills** needed to implement the countermeasure. For example, a skilled carpenter is needed to fit the door. I do not have the skills so I have employed John to do the job.
- **Impact** on the family and house of implementing the countermeasure. For example, having no front door for half a day while it is replaced. It is summer and I can work at home that day so the impact is minimal.
- The **overall benefits** that will be gained by implementing the countermeasure. For example, total security from a professionally installed door and frame, with new locks, a door viewer and hinge bolts. This door will be totally secure, and will have the benefits of a secure letterbox, mail basket, internal flap and built in letterbox draught excluder.
- You should also remember that increased security could give **financial benefits** as well, because insurance companies may reduce insurance premiums when double-glazing and multi-point locking external doors are fitted.

If you have too many countermeasures to easily cope with, or the sorting process causes you any difficulty, do the sorting in stages. For example, take each item and sort them into different piles (I) Immediate, (S) Soon, (I&W) If & When possible, and (NS) Non-Security. Then carefully review and sort each problem in each pile separately.

- **Immediate**. This list will contain all actions that you consider should be completed urgently. This could include such actions as replacing the faulty front door lock, which is clearly an urgent item, but this list might include apparently 'non-urgent' items. For example, you may have realised that the bushes at the front of the house have grown too high and you have listed a countermeasure to cut them back. That is hardly an 'urgent' countermeasure, but because you can easily cut back the bushes, it will only take half an hour and cost nothing, it can be done in the next few days when you have half an hour to spare, so it appears on the immediate list.
- **Soon.** This list contains all of the actions that you consider should be completed soon, but are not classified as immediate. For example, you may want to replace the locks and bolts on the garage door. Due to the cost, you decide not to do that until next month (when you are due to get a new car and a ride-on mower, which will both be kept in the garage).
- **If and when possible.** This classification contains the actions that deliver the 'nice to have' countermeasures. For example, a state of the art, monitored burglar alarm system would be nice to have. It would increase household security immeasurably, but at a price of £3,000 with a £200 a year monitoring fee, due to our financial circumstances it will have to wait on the 'if and when possible' list.
- **Non-security.** This list contains countermeasures that are not directly related to security, but which you would be foolish to ignore. For example, you may have spotted a loose slate when performing the perimeter survey, or noticed that the header tank in the loft that feeds the central heating system appears to be corroded. These defects, risks and problems cannot be ignored. You must take steps to address them, and the non-security list is the mechanism through which you manage them. Such things as water pipes not being lagged, or the absence of a smoke detector on the upstairs landings will also be added to this list. Don't forget these issues; even though they are not strictly security issues, you must address them.

Example prioritisation

When you have completed the listing process, you have to sort the counter-measures into priority order. The process is straightforward, though not necessarily simple. You will have to consider all factors to define a priority order. To illustrate the process and the sort of factors you will have to consider in assigning priorities, assume we have been presented with an unusually manageable list of four countermeasures. They were simply listed in the order we identified them; as yet they are in no particular order.

- Cut down shrubs in front garden.
- Replace broken front door lock.
- Renew old front door.
- Ensure house always locked when we leave.

I have prioritised these four actions as shown below. Beside each action is an explanation of my thought process, describing why I decided to rank the actions the way I did.

Prioritised actions	Explanation as to why the countermeasures were placed in this priority order
1) Everyone to agree to ensure that the house is always locked when we leave.	The only people who live in our house are my wife and I. While doing the security survey we realised we are sometimes a little careless about household security, for example not locking up if we are 'only nipping down to the shops'. We have already recognised the risk we have been taking and have already agreed always to lock and secure the house if we are both out. This action was agreed, and completed over breakfast this morning!
2) Cut down shrubs in front garden.	Neither of us are gardeners and we have avoided tackling the front garden. Originally we didn't think it mattered if the bushes got a little tall. We now realise that our ragged front garden could help burglars to raid our house. The shops are shut at the moment which means that we cannot tackle any other countermeasures on the priority list, so we may as well go out and cut the bushes back now before it gets too dark. Another day at another time this countermeasure would be lower priority but due

	to current circumstances, it is the highest priority because it is all we can do at this time, and we have the skills and free time to do it.
3) Replace broken front door lock.	The front door lock has been temperamental for some time, but we have put off getting it fixed because we intend to get a completely new front door at some stage. We now realise that having a secure front door is important and putting off getting the new lock is a mistake. As soon as the shops open tomorrow we will buy and fit a new lock; after all, when we get a new front door John the carpenter says he can use that new lock on the new door.
4) Renew old front door.	The old front door is warped and lets a draught in. In a westerly wind the door lets in rainwater too, but we don't often get a westerly wind. There is some rot at the bottom of the door, but it is adequate for now. I don't have the skills and tools needed to fit a new door, so we will have to pay for it to be done and hope to have it done in the next month. John the carpenter says he will come and do it for us but we are waiting to be paid for some overtime we did at work to get the money to buy the new door and pay John to fit it.

Given your skills, abilities and wealth, you might have prioritised the example actions listed above in a different order. That is perfectly acceptable, because the whole point of this method and process is to tailor the reviews, actions and countermeasures to your personal circumstances.

For example, you might have put replacing the front door first, because in your case you are a carpenter, the front door is badly rotted and the frame is coming away from the wall. A new lock under those circumstances would have been a waste of time!

Revisit and revise the priorities

Though you arrive at a prioritisation list, that may not reflect the order in which countermeasures are completed. For example, putting a top and bottom bolt in the inside of the tool shed double doors (where the bolts will secure the double door and make them stronger) may be the lowest priority countermeasure we have on our list. Replacing the front door might be the highest priority item on that same list. However, circumstances may dictate the order in which they are completed. Perhaps we have already started to tackle the highest priority countermeasures – we ordered a new UPVC steel framed front door on the day we completed our survey. Unfortunately, there is a four-week delay in delivering and installing that new, high priority, secure, weatherproof, steel framed, UPVC front door.

In the meantime we can carry on tackling the other, possibly lower priority countermeasures on the list, because we have the time and or skills to do so. Perhaps we had an hour spare last Sunday so we fitted the new bolts on the shed door and finished that 'low priority' countermeasure two and a half weeks before the high priority new front door is installed.

Just as long as you attempt to address the items in priority order, resolving the worst risks and issues as soon as you can, the order in which they are completed doesn't really matter. But where there is a choice of completing a low priority or a high priority action today, always aim to deliver the high priority countermeasure.

Prioritisation considerations

There are many factors that could affect your decision as to how to prioritise items. A few examples are given below, with a brief explanation.

Considerations	Explanation/examples of why an action may be delayed
Money	If you cannot afford to do it, it will have to wait.
Time available	If you don't have time it will have to wait.
Skills/knowledge	If you don't know how to do it, or lack some special skills, the action will have to wait until that issue is resolved.
Tools/equipment	If you don't have specialist tools and equipment required to be able to finish a job, it will have to wait until you do.
Weather/season	If some work required to tackle an action has to be done in warm or dry weather, it cannot be done in mid-winter.
Planning rules	If you need to apply for planning permission before you can build a porch or replace windows, the job will have to wait.
Assistance	If a job needs two people to do it safely, then it will have to wait until you can arrange for somebody to help.

There will undoubtedly be other pressures and restrictions that are unique to you! For example, you may be disabled and can only do things that are possible in a wheelchair, or you may live on an island and some problems can only be addressed at low tide! You will have to make your best efforts to resolve issues and outstanding actions when you can.

You should also remember that some countermeasures have been listed on the 'if and when possible' list. For example, replacing the footpath and drive with gravel doesn't need to be done immediately. Having had a quote of £1,675 to do the job it is probably not even justifiable, but if in two or five years' time the drive needs resurfacing perhaps you can resurrect this action and take the gravel option for your new drive, with security in mind.

The main point to remember is, since you took the time to identify security issues relating to your house, you must make any changes you can justify and achieve, but don't lose sight of outstanding issues. Keep them in mind, regularly review them and resolve any outstanding issues to deliver selected counter-measures when you can.

When you define the actions necessary to implement a countermeasure, they may seem very simple. For example, getting everyone to agree to make sure the house is secure when they go out costs nothing. It only needs agreement from everyone so it could take just a few minutes to complete. It needs no extra skills or equipment so that should be marked 'Immediate priority' and be assigned to the immediate list.

However, perhaps two members of the family are on a hiking holiday some-where in Europe so it cannot be done immediately. There isn't any way of contacting the hikers to discuss the problem and seek agreement, so this counter-measure may be listed as 'soon', knowing it can easily be completed when the family gets together in two months' time!

There may still be little things that you can do. For example, get everyone who is living in the house to agree always to lock the door, and to stop and check to see if the door is locked before they leave. A little extra security could be gained by putting a sign inside each door, saying something like 'Check Door Is Locked'.

Getting somebody to lag the pipes in the loft and check that crusty looking stopcock will be on the (NS) 'non-security' list, as would the installation of smoke detectors.

Mark the four categories on the top of four flip chart pages: (I) Immediate, (S) Soon, (I & W) If & When possible, and (NS) Non-Security. With the headed pages set up, work through your actions, write each of them on a new sticky note and stick it to the appropriate flip chart page.

Action Lists

When you have listed the countermeasures you propose to implement, you may want to compile an action list for each countermeasure. The action list is simply a list of the tasks you have to complete to implement the stated countermeasure. Tasks are usually listed in the order they need to be completed to deliver the countermeasure. If the countermeasure is to fit a new bulb in the porch light, you won't need to bother to create an action list, but where the countermeasure is more complicated an action list will be a huge help.

Example action list

Taking as an example the countermeasure of 'standardise house identification in our street', you have to look at the tasks and actions that you will need to complete in order to standardise house identification in your street.

The action list will show each of the steps needed to do that, in the order in which they have to be completed. When finished, the action list becomes a plan, check list and work schedule that will help you to introduce that countermeasure.

A possible action list of the steps and tasks needed to introduce standardised house identification in your street might be:

1. Research the availability, style, size, durability, design and cost of house name signs.
2. Research the methods of attaching, mounting and positioning house name signs for optimum visibility.
3. Investigate the possibility of discounts if everyone in the street buys a sign from the same company.
4. Check to make sure that the most appropriate sign and mounting system will work on every property in the road.
5. Discuss the proposal with fire, police and ambulance personnel and record their support and comments.
6. Find a local handyman who could install all of the signs if required to do so, and list the price he will charge. Negotiate a discount for multiple signs/houses.
7. Make a presentation to remind the residents' committee of the risks and dangers that could be associated with emergency services staff being unable to find any given house. Describe the problems your friend had in finding your house when you undertook a test. Stress the difficulty of finding one house in the dark and rain, and explain how that could affect the security and health of everyone in the street.

8. Make a presentation of your research into signs. Present a few samples. Present the cost savings residents will make by taking advantage of the discounts you have negotiated. Describe the response of representatives of the emergency services to the standardised sign initiative.
9. Request that residents association members should vote on the initiative.
10. If accepted, be ready with a form for all members to write in their house name and or number, for a centralised bulk order. Take the money from members as they fill in the form so that the initiative can be completed without further delay.
11. Take delivery of the new signs and mounting brackets, etc.
12. Arrange with the handyman to fit all of the signs.

When all of those steps have been successfully completed, the countermeasure is in place. As with this example action list, in some cases the necessary steps and actions could take some weeks to complete.

Action list considerations

The action list will also help you to understand the effort, cost and time required to implement your countermeasures. Compiling the action list allows you to break down tasks required to manageable and understandable proportions.

For each task you can look at the time, cost, skills required and impact of the task. Noting them against the actions, you can soon define total cost, time required for delivery, specialist skills required and any impacts and knock-on effects.

Using the above example the table below indicates the results you may get from this exercise.

SR1/27 Standardise house names and identification for Badger Road					
No	Action	Cost	Time	Skills	Impact
1	Research availability style, size, durability, design and cost of house name signs	Nil	10 days	Internet Directory Phone	Nil
2	Research attaching, mounting and positioning house name signs for optimum visibility	Nil	5 days	Advice Police and Builder	Possibly need to erect posts at some houses

3	Investigate discounts if everyone in the street buys a sign from the same company.	Nil	10 days	Get quotes	Nil
4	Check to make sure that the most appropriate sign and mounting system will work on every property in the road.	Nil	1 day	Check each property	Extra work may be required at some houses.
5	Discuss the proposal with fire, police and ambulance personnel.	Nil	5 days	Nil	They think it is such a good idea they want to write about it in their newsletters and staff magazines.
6	Find a local handyman who could install all of the signs. Negotiate discount.	Nil	5 days	Nil	Nil
7	Make a presentation to the residents' association, explain problems, stress benefits.	Nil	1 hour	Nil	Nil
8	Make a presentation of your research into signs. Present a few samples. Present the cost savings from discounts negotiated.	Nil	1 hour	Nil	Nil
9	Request that residents' association members should vote on the initiative.	Nil	10 mins	Nil	Nil or authorisation to order the sign and work to begin.

10	If accepted, issue form and collect money.	£1 to print forms.	15 mins	Nil
11	Take delivery of the new signs and mounting brackets, etc.	Nil	1 day	Nil
12	Arrange with the handyman to fit all of the signs.	£10 per house	Nil	Nil

In this case, the table shows us that there is almost no cost involved in preparing to implement this countermeasure. There will be costs in buying the signs and having them erected, but there should be a group discount on that.

The time required seems rather long! It adds up to a total of 37 days, 2 hours and 25 minutes. But there are several factors that you have to remember in this instance.

- Because the long-term goal is to make each house in the street easily identifiable at any time, a lead-time of a month or so may be quite acceptable.
- Most of the time allocated is for research into the availability of signs, talking to the emergency services to prove that the exercise will be worthwhile, etc. Remember this is a background task for one resident, and we had to build in enough time for enquiries to be made and for quotes to come back through the post.
- Lastly, we have to look at the sequence:
  - ➤ Action 1 is to research availability and cost of signs.
  - ➤ Action 2 is to research method of erecting those signs. The company providing the signs probably also provides posts and fixings, and will advise on that at the same time, depending on the type of signs selected. That means that actions 1 and 2 can possibly be run in parallel.
  - ➤ Action 3 is to research possible discounts, which means we may as well add that enquiry when we first talk to the sign companies we approach. Tell them that there are 35 houses in our road, and ask what discounts they will offer if each household buys a sign and fixings. This means that to a large extent action 3 can run in parallel with actions 1 and 2.
  - ➤ Action 4 is to check to see that the same mounting system will work on each house in the street. That is listed to take a day, and we should be able to do

153

that quite early in the process. By looking at the signs available, we can see and list the common fixing methods. While we are waiting for the formal quotes from the sign companies we can check the houses in the street to make sure that the fixing methods will work on all properties. That means that this action could be completed before actions 1, 2, and 3 are completed so they will all run in parallel.

➢ Action 5 is to discuss the initiative with the emergency services. After a few days, we should have a good idea of the type of sign and fixing method, so we can approach the emergency services and talk to them about what we are planning. Anything that helps them to find properties will be welcomed, and in the case above, they are so pleased with the initiative that they have said they are going to write about it in their newsletters and suggest that other communities follow our example!

➢ Actions 7, 8, 9 and 10 take only a short time at the next residents' association meeting.

➢ Action 11 takes one day because the company offers next day delivery!

➢ That means that although the total time added up to 37 days 2 hours and 25 minutes, in reality with a bit of luck we can actually probably introduce this countermeasure and the handyman can start putting the new signs up within a couple of weeks!

No special skills are required, and the only impact is that if the residents vote yes, the signs will have to be ordered and the workman contracted to erect them.

The details for each action could include:

- **Time** – how long (measured in hours) it will take to introduce the counter-measure.
- **Cost** – how much it will cost to introduce the countermeasure, including all costs, such as buying materials, renting tools and equipment or paying a professional to do it.
- **Skills** – are any special skills required for you to introduce a given counter-measure? For example, you may need an electrician.
- **Impacts** – you must decide what impacts, if any, the new countermeasure will have on your house, family or lifestyle. For example, will you have to move out while electricians lift floorboards to rewire the house and install a combination burglar alarm and fire alarm system?

Additional sample action lists are given below.

Badger View – 'New front door' action list		
Countermeasure	**Actions**	**Priority**
Fit new front door *Time* – 4 hrs for carpenter to intall it *Cost* – £145 for door, £78 for door furniture, preparation and labour £195 *Skills* – carpenter with experience of locks and other security devices. *Impact* – door will be removed for 4 hours, somebody will have to be at home that day.	1) Speak to John the carpenter we use to explain the requirement. 2) Select a door from the range John has available. 3) Select locks and security devices on advice from John. 4) Select other door furniture such as letterbox, doorbell, door viewer etc. 5) Check and approve final total cost with John. 6) Arrange date for work to be done. Book that day off work. 7) Remove keys and furniture from front hall so that John has room to work. 8) Watch what John does to confirm that he is doing what was asked and that nobody sneaks into the house wile the front door is removed.	**IMMEDIATE** The exising front door is rotten, the frame is loose and two front door keys cannot be found.

Badger View – Non-security – 'Loft plumbing' action list		
Countermeasure	**Actions**	**Priority**
Lag pipes in loft *Time* – 1 hour. *Cost* – £12 to buy lagging material. *Skills* – none needed. *Impact* – none.	1) Buy DIY pack of pipe lagging. 2) Fit lagging to the pipes that are not lagged.	**IMMEDIATE** It is autumn, long range forecasts predict very cold weather next month. It would be foolish not to do the job this weekend.

Accidents at Home

In the first chapter we defined security as the application of methods and procedures that are used to make our lifestyle secure against any vulnerabilities, threats and risks, where by applying security appropriately, we will achieve safety!

Accidents in the home are therefore a threat to our safety and security, in its broadest sense. We will take a brief look at accident prevention in the home. Statistics show that a majority of injuries are caused by accidents inside the home and those accidents are responsible for a lot of domestic injuries and fatalities.

The causes and effects of the accidents could probably be listed under a few headings:

- **Falls/slips/trips.** These include stairs, loose carpet, trailing shoelaces, toys (left on stairs and steps), trailing wires, loose floorboards, using inappropriate items to climb to reach high objects (climbing onto a stool instead of using a ladder), small dogs (running under the feet of an elderly person) and wet floors, oil spillage, etc.
- **Burns/scalds.** These include spills or misuse of boiling water, food (hot drinks and soup), cooking oil, household chemicals (getting bleach and other caustic materials onto the hands), hot utensils (burns from cooking dishes), etc.
- **Poisoning.** This includes gas (faulty gas appliances, blocked air vents, faulty devices, poor installation and maintenance), misuse of household and garden chemicals (child drinks weed killer kept in lemonade bottle), etc.
- **Cuts.** These include cuts from broken glass, a knife in the spoon tray (fumbling for a spoon cut fingers on knife), misuse of knives and tools (using a knife as a screwdriver, misusing a wood chisel (gouging towards yourself instead of away) and carelessness (cutting your hand as you open a baked bean tin), etc.
- **Electrocution.** Often caused by tampering with electrical wiring and equipment, such as attempting to repair a vacuum cleaner or other faulty device. Can be caused by unskilled attempts to install or amend electrical wiring; can also be caused by misuse and lack of care of existing electrical circuits and equipment. Always instal and use a power leakage circuit breaker to protect you, particularly when using electrical equipment outside the house.
- **Explosions.** Caused by misuse of gas and or flammable fluids, for example exposing a naked flame when there is a gas leak or perhaps careless storage or use of petrol (or other flammable liquids) in a garage or workshop.
- **Fire.** Can be caused by some of the above behaviour and activity. Could also be caused by careless disposal of cigarettes, carelessness with the use of gas and

electric fires indoors, careless use of a paraffin heater, or lack of care and common sense when burning rubbish or letting off fireworks.

- **Machinery injury.** Many injuries are caused by misuse of home machinery. For example, garden equipment (lawn mowers, garden shredders, hedge trimmers, chain saws), vehicles (cars, vans, motorcycles), kitchen equipment (blenders, waste disposal units), electrical tools (drills, planes or disk cutters).
- **Combination.** Any of the above causes could act in combination, for example misuse of an electric drill when repairing a car, causing fuel to leak, which in turn causes an explosion and fire.

Knowing the range of accidents that can occur in and around the home, we should all take extra care. Why make the home as secure from crime as you can and then allow yourself and family members to be injured or killed by stupid accidents? Countermeasures are simple:

Accidents at home – countermeasures

✔ Wear recommended safety equipment, such as safety glasses, gloves and steel toecap shoes or boots.

✔ Read, understand and follow all instructions for any tool, equipment or activity.

✔ Make sure that safety guards and safety equipment are in use at all times.

✔ If you are not sure how to do it, or have any safety concerns, stop – don't do it, seek advice, guidance and or training.

✔ Make sure that any working area is clear of obstructions or hazards before starting on anything.

✔ Take all safety measures seriously, never take any shortcuts – for example, always turn off the electricity, and check to see that it is off before changing a plug or touching any electrical circuit.

✔ Always ensure that all tools and equipment are in perfect working order before trying to use them.

✔ Always warn anyone else who is around when you are starting a job, and if necessary erect protective barriers.

✔ Before doing anything in which there is a potential element of risk, stop and reconsider. Make sure that everything is ready before you start.

✔ As a general rule, make sure that your living and working areas are clean, clear and tidy.

8 In Perspective

We have discussed criminals and the ways they target us. We have discussed some statistics and reports on the level and value of crime, but I want to take a moment to try to put all of this into perspective.

Crime Levels

Generally the front pages of newspapers are the only source of information that the average person has on the level of crime. Unfortunately newspapers are sold by what is on the front page. They rely on people buying the paper to read the story behind the front page picture or headline. That of course means that editors are motivated to make the front page as spectacular and as lurid as possible, because if they do they will sell more papers.

Newspapers often give the impression that society has broken down and that we live in a time of urban warfare between criminal armies and helpless citizens. However, crime levels are nowhere near as bad as most people think!

There is a high and increasing level of crime in this country. Vehicle crime and burglary seem to be climbing steeply, but statistically the *average person* is unlikely to be affected by it.

The more you can do to protect yourself from crime by removing vulnerabilities and avoiding risks and threats, the less likely you are to be affected by crime.

When you have worked through this book, your eye and thought processes should have been educated to allow you to see potential threats. That will allow you to identify countermeasures and changes that will reduce or remove those threats.

REMEMBER if the *average* person is statistically unlikely to be the victim of a crime, reading and acting on the advice and information in this book will make you *highly unlikely* to be the victim of crime

The Value of Statistics

When most people see a report, they unquestioningly accept the statistics that are shown. They seem to be official, scientific and therefore trustworthy!

The reality is they may be, but they may not be. Will Rogers once said: 'There are lies, damn lies and statistics.' I don't think I would go that far in condemning all statistics, but I have seen occasions where officially released statistics have been misleading if not blatantly wrong.

Wrong question

As an absolutely ludicrous example, I recently saw the officially published results of a survey. The report heading stated '97% of employees victim of assault'.

That grabbed my attention so I took the time to read through it. I couldn't help digging further to find out where this hotbed of violence was. In doing so I found that the results were invalid, and the report heading was sensationalist with no founding at all in the statistics that had been produced.

In part of the survey they had asked employees 'Have you or a colleague been the victim of an assault during the last 12 months?' With that as a survey question, in my opinion any results collected were clearly worthless, and any conclusions drawn from the survey results were therefore totally invalid.

Allow me to explain in case you missed it. Take a moment to consider that survey question. To make the mathematics easier, let's assume that 100 people work in the establishment where the survey was taken. They are then asked that question, 'Have you or a colleague been the victim of an assault during the last 12 months?'

If in 'scenario A', 11 months and 29 days before the survey was taken, one single employee had been pushed once by a customer, all of the staff at that company would have to answer 'yes', because they *'or a colleague'* had been the victim of violence during the past year.

Statistically that is 100%. Assume a few members of staff were on holiday when the survey was taken or didn't bother responding and we have 97% of staff answering yes. Exactly like the published survey behind that frantic newspaper headline.

In 'scenario B', almost the opposite could be true. Using the same assumed 100 employees, perhaps in this case every one of the employees had personally been the victim of violence on a weekly basis over the past year.

That adds up to one assault per employee per week = 5,200 assaults over the last year. When the survey is taken a few employees are still in hospital recovering from their latest assault so there is only a 97% response rate.

In both scenario A and scenario B, statistically and correctly there is a 97% affirmative response, but because of the loose wording of the question the reality behind that is radically different. In scenario A, there was only one minor assault almost a year ago, and in scenario B, 5,200 assaults over the past year, 100 assaults per week!

Right question

Let's take another look at that survey. What if we change the question to 'Have you *personally* been the victim of assault at work during the last year?' That is more specific and definite, we can't go wrong with that, can we? Have you been assaulted – yes or no? So what would you think if I told you I had been out and asked 100 people that question with the result that 43% stated that they had been assaulted at work during the last 12 months?

That is terrible. Nearly half of the people I asked have personally been assaulted at work within the last year. There is no confusion over the question, it was them, they were assaulted, not a friend or colleague or relative! The results clearly show that 43 out of a hundred had been assaulted. That sounds really bad, there are obviously an awful lot of people getting assaulted at work!

Wrong place

But wait – we're suspicious about surveys and statistics now. The question looks good, no ambiguity there. What else can we find out about the survey?

What if I told you it was taken in a hospital casualty unit in the night club area of a major city at 11 on a Friday night? Does the statistical integrity still stand? Could it be that we got such a high number of employee assaults because we are taking the survey in a place where victims of assaults tend to gather? Would it help to admit that three quarters of those employees were security staff and bouncers from the clubs and pubs around town? Would we have got the same results if we had taken the survey outside the library at ten o'clock on a Sunday morning?

Wrong question – again

Could we have asked the wrong question as well? It is possible to ask a leading question or phrase a question in such a way that we will get the answer we want. As a silly example to tie in with our assault at work survey, I might engineer a 'yes' reply with the same question but the following introduction.

'Hello. I am trying to get the government to cut income tax. We think that too many people are getting assaulted at work and if we can prove that in this survey, the government will cut income tax by 5%, which means that the average person will be £100 a week better off. So could you tell me please *have you personally been the victim of assault at work during the last year?*'

What? A tax cut if I've been assaulted at work in the last year – sure, I've been assaulted a half a dozen times (when do I get the £1,200?).

We could take another approach with the same question but engineer a negative response.

'Hello. Sorry to waste your time but I'm asking real men about assaults at work. Apparently weak, scared, spineless men are claiming that they have been assaulted at work. We want to know the truth so we are asking real men *have you personally been the victim of assault at work during the last year?*'

Weak? Scared? Spineless? No mate, not me, I've never been assaulted, nobody would dare to try to assault me!

Questioning statistics

So, as we have seen, statistics – especially those concerning levels of crime – are open to question. They may not be as reliable as the newspaper scare stories would have us believe.

9 Conclusion

You are extremely unlikely to be involved in headline grabbing and exotic crimes. Though some crime is increasing, you can avoid it by being sensible, maintaining awareness of your security and surroundings and taking simple steps to protect yourself.

Common Sense

A good level of security is quite easy to achieve when you know how. Good security is based on:

- You remaining aware of your surroundings.
- Recognising everything that is happening around you, particularly anything that could develop in a way that could affect you, your property or your loved ones.
- Recognising vulnerabilities that could leave you open to threats and risks.
- Proactively addressing vulnerabilities to remove them or reduce them to an acceptable level.
- Identifying and assessing the threat posed by potential risks as they develop and taking steps to avoid those risks or taking steps to reduce their impact to acceptable levels.
- Taking common sense steps to protect yourself and your property, such as:
  ➢ Don't go out and get drunk, drunks are far more likely to become the victim of theft, robbery, assault and other crimes and to commit crimes such as theft, criminal damage and assaults.
  ➢ Don't leave valuables visible in an unattended car.
  ➢ Never leave your keys in your car.
  ➢ Don't be careless, keep your handbag, purse, wallet and other portable valuables with you or locked securely away.

➢ Make sure that your house is as secure as you can make it.

➢ Be cautious with visitors who want to come into the house.

➢ Be cautious when disclosing personal information, in forms, on the Internet, when ordering and when using your credit cards.

➢ Shred personal documents, don't let the criminals steal your identity.

Don't Worry Too Much

Don't ruin your life by devoting your whole existence to 'staying safe'. Don't believe the scare stories you see on the television and the front pages of the newspapers, just learn the lessons that apply to you and your life.

Don't allow yourself to become preoccupied with types and levels of crime, that do not concern you and will never affect you.

Security awareness should be a natural and automatic part of your lifestyle just as much as safely crossing the road. You have trained yourself not to cross a road without looking, and that has become an automatic part of your life.

You don't constantly worry about roads and traffic. You don't walk around in fear of cars, or of becoming the victim of a traffic accident. You have learned and developed the skill of crossing a road safely when you need to. That has become embedded in your lifestyle, you automatically identify a road, then automatically call up and use the safe road crossing method you have learned.

I suggest that security can be a similar 'automatic' skill, given guidance and practice.

Remember that just by considering your security and taking the simplest measures you are far less likely to become a victim of crime. Don't be gullible stay alert, review your security when you need to, take appropriate countermeasures where you can and you will have a safe, secure and happy life.

Useful Websites

The Internet makes a world of information available to everyone. Some people may think that they are excluded because they do not have a home computer or advanced computer skills, but they are wrong.

There are a wide range of places and organisations where you can access the Internet. From coffee shops with Internet computers available for the public to use, to libraries, colleges and schools. Most also offer support and training to those who need it. If you want to learn how to use the Internet, ask in your local library first – even if they don't offer training, they should be able to give you a list of places that do.

If you are nervous about using the Internet for the first time, don't worry – most people are surprised at how easy it is. By the time the average person has had a little practice, they usually say that they don't know why they were so nervous in the first place!

I have only mentioned a few websites in this book, because a world of information that is specific to your own personal needs and circumstances is freely available to you on the Internet. Use a search engine such as Google (www.google.co.uk) or (www.ask.co.uk) to find information on almost anything.

The sites I have mentioned are:

Flooding Information – the Environment Agency

www.environment-agency.gov.uk
The Environment Agency website allows you to type in a postcode and check flooding maps, which will give you a good idea of the risk of flooding for any given location and property.

Crime statistics

www.crimestatistics.org.uk

Various Internet sources are available for you to check crime figures in an area.

This one allows you to check on a postcode basis. Some local authorities and other organisations also hold information about crime rates and trends.

Tool and door and window locks

www.screwfix.com
Locks and fitting are available from good hardware stores. Those illustrated are shown courtesy of Screwfix, a large company which sells tools, materials and fittings. They offer national coverage and can provide next day delivery.

Stolen property searches

The police have their own databases that they can search to identify stolen property, but there are some databases that are available for the public to use. These include:
www.trace.co.uk
www.virtualbumblebee.co.uk

Stopping unwanted mail, fax and telephone advertising

If you want to try to stop, or at least reduce the amount of unsolicited advertising you receive by mail, fax and telephone, visiting the following sites to register your details. It will take a few months to work and isn't guaranteed to stop all junk mail, but it helps.

Facsimile Preference Service

www.fpsonline.org.uk
You can register your fax number and state that you do not want unsolicited fax advertising material.

Mail Preference Service

www.mpsonline.org.uk
You can register your address and state that you do not want unsolicited advertising material through the post.

Telephone Preference Service

www.tpsonline.org.uk
You can register your phone number and state that you do not want unsolicited phone calls.

Index